PUNCH CRAZY

PUNCHNEEDLE EMBROIDERY WITH CRAZY PATCHWORK

Pamela Gurney

 AUSSIE PUBLISHERS

ACKNOWLEDGEMENTS

With love to my ever-loving and patient family, who through rain, hail and shine, make their way to my studio with cups of coffee to keep me going. This is the second book in two years and I'm not sure they will be so tolerant again, for a while.

To my many friends who give me loving support and gentle encouragement when they know I am tucked away in my studio on a mission. Teri, this book would not have happened without you sorting out my computer problems and making a back-up copy for 'just in case' when indeed we lost everything from the hard drive!

To my dear friends and photographers, Robina and Tony. Thank you from my heart.

I know I drive you crazy, Leo (Scott), but you also know that I appreciate your framing skills. And to Alison McNicholl who so beautifully makes up my cushions.

Thank you to Craft Australia for their initiative with the Craftmark Australia campaign. Recognition and accreditation with the Craftmark logo of my textile art, incorporating the relatively unknown medium of punchneedle embroidery, encourages me to share the potential of a very old, almost forgotten needle art.

Thank you to Pepin Press, Holland, who have allowed me to use some insect designs from their 'Designs of Nature". Thank you also to my dear friend Annabelle and her colleague Simon, who put so much time and effort into preparing my artwork for printing.

Daryl Craze, from Aussie Publishers, has had the courage to support me with this largely unknown form of embroidery. Without his belief that I had the knowledge and indeed a gift which I had to share with others, neither of my books would have come to fruition. Thank you to everyone else at Aussie Publishers for your kindness and help over the past few years.

AUSSIE PUBLISHERS

25-27 Izett Street, Prahran Victoria 3181 Australia

Web site: http://www.penguin-threads.com.au

E-mail: info@penguin-threads.com.au

First published by Aussie Publishers 1999

10 9 8 7 6 5 4 3 2 1

Text, patterns and designs copyright © Pamela Gurney

Photography copyright © Robina and Tony Summers

This compilation copyright © Aussie Publishers, 1999

All rights reserved.

Designed and produced by Borghesi & Adam Publishers Pty. Ltd.

Printed and bound in Singapore.

National Library of Australia Cataloguing-in-Publication Data:

Gurney, Pamela.

Punch Crazy : punchneedle embroidery with crazy patchwork

ISBN 1 876 364 97 1

1. Punched work. 2. Embroidery. I. Title.

746.44

Contents

Acknowledgements 2

Introduction 5

Equipment 7

   Punchneedles 7

   Threaders 9

   Gauges 9

   Fabric 9

   Iron-on Interfacing 10

   Hoops 11

   Threads 11

   Magic Pen (Madeira) 12

   Iron-on Transfer Pencil 12

   Dressmaker's Carbon 12

   Scissors 13

   Tweezers 13

   Ruler 13

   Crochet Hook 13

   Razor Blade 13

   Patterns and Designs 13

   Glue 14

Techniques 15

   Transferring the Design 15

   Placing the Fabric in the Hoop 15

   Pile Depth 16

   Conversion Chart 18

   Marking the Straight Grain onto Fabric 19

   Care of Punchneedles 19

   Threading the Punchneedle 19

   Stitching with your Punchneedles 20

   Cutting Threads 23

   What Keeps the Loops in Place 23

   Posture 24

   Problems and Solutions 25

   Applique of a Design 27

   To Glue or Not to Glue 28

   Choosing the Size of Fabric 29

   Washing 29

   Pressing 29

Embroidery Guide 31

   Special Effects 31

   Normal Punchneedle Embroidery 31

   Reverse Punchneedle Embroidery 34

   Counting Stitches 36

Crazy Patchwork 45

   Method for a Crazy Patchwork Block 46

   Embroidery for Crazy Patchwork 47

Projects ....

   A Paler Shade of Crazy 48

   Colour Me Crazy 50

   Crazy Night 53

   Crazy with Fragrance 58

   Bear in a Crazy Patch 63

   Elegantly Crazy 70

   Crazy Angel Fish 76

   Crazy but Cozy 81

   Crazy About Christmas 85

Patterns 89

The completed cushion from Crazy About Christmas,

(see page 85).

Introduction

Punchneedle embroidery has intrigued and excited me for many years. I love creating new designs and textures with my punchneedles. I also enjoy crazy patchwork and find it a wonderful canvas upon which to work the magic of punchneedle embroidery. It is an ideal way for me to combine two forms of needle art which I love.

In this book I concentrate on bringing to you the varied ways I have found to use my punchneedles to embellish a piece of crazy patchwork, and to bring a plain piece of fabric to life. I offer many new and exciting designs, which can be taken and used anywhere you want. For instance, use the individual designs on shirt collars, pockets, cushions and children's clothes, or frame them.

I only briefly touch on the piecing of crazy patchwork as there are many wonderful books available that give an A-to-Z on how to work this form of patchwork and the associated surface stitches used with it.

The colours and textures which can be incorporated into a piece of embroidery by using punchneedles thrill me. I marvel at the versatility of work which can be achieved from the simple stitch worked with the punchneedle. They are truly 'dancing needles'.

It is through my 'dancing needles', and my great enjoyment of crazy patchwork and punchneedle embroidery, that this book comes to you. I am delighted to be able to share both of them with you. Please enjoy!

Pamela

1 punchneedle (type 1)
2 punchneedle (type 2)
3 threader (type 1)
4 threader (type 2)
5 crochet hook
6 tweezers
7 my first book
8 Madeira Glamour thread
9 Madeira Decora thread

10 Appleton's tapestry wool
11 Appleton's crewel wool
12 rayon ribbon
13 Madeira machine embroidery thread
14 Madeira Silk thread
15 Madeira Decora thread
16 Madeira Stranded Cotton

17 Madeira Metallic thread
18 Madeira Metallic thread
19 You Can Wash It glue
20 Off 'N On glue
21 lead pencil
22 iron-on transfer pencil
23 Madeira Magic pen
24 small ruler and razor blade
25 razor blade

26 embroidery scissors
27 plastic gauge
28 slant scissors
29 silk ribbon
30 assorted hoops
31 assorted fabrics
32 iron-on woven interfacing
33 calico

Equipment

In punchneedle embroidery, a special needle is used to punch thread and ribbons through fabric which is held tightly in a hoop. A pattern is traced onto the back of the fabric which the embroiderer follows. By using the punching technique, loops are formed on the front of the fabric, creating a beautiful textured finish. The loops can be trimmed and shaped to give many different textural effects.

PUNCHNEEDLES

Generally, a punchneedle will combine a needle made from stainless steel, surgical steel, brass and other types of metal with a handle made from brass, plastic, wood or Bakelite. The needle and handle are hollow, allowing thread to be passed through them. The needle tip has a bevelled or slanted edge on one side and the other side is straight. The eye of the punchneedle is bored through the straight side of the needle.

Above: A variety of punchneedles

There is a wide range of punchneedles available *(see the photograph on page 7)*. I experiment with the many which I come across, or which are lent to me by the generous people I meet when I am sharing this beautiful art. I have quite a collection of my own, ranging from large, for rug-making, to the curious, such as one made from a very fine hypodermic needle with a piece of plastic for a handle. With some experimentation and adaptation, most punchneedles can be used to re-create my designs.

I meet many people who see me working and they say, 'When I was a child, my mother/grandmother/father used to make rugs like that, but with a bigger needle.' I always ask if they have any samples left in their homes. Sadly, because of the utilitarian nature of these rugs everyone tells me they no longer exist. If you have one of these old, hand-punched rugs, treasure it.

Like sewing machines, all punchneedles work on the same principle, but some will be able to do more or less than others. Having a couple of different types will be an advantage. Some sets have one very fine punchneedle; others have a large punchneedle which allows you to do beautiful ribbon work.

You will be able to get the most from your needles if you give time to experimenting and practice. I realise this is annoying when all you want to do is to get on with a design. However, if you are anything like me, when you start a design and it doesn't work you will put it aside and never finish it. After many years of doing this I realised that some preparation takes away that failure and frustration.

I particularly like working fine embroidery. There are some designs in this book which have been specifically worked with a very fine punchneedle with only one strand of thread. These same designs can be enlarged and worked with a larger punchneedle using more strands of thread. I urge you to experiment with your punchneedles and the designs which I have worked for this book. I hope they are an inspiration to you and allow you to realise what a wonderful needleworking tool you have in your embroidery basket.

There are two different sets of punchneedles that I use *(see the photograph on page 6):* The first set (No. 1 in the photograph) has three different-sized punchneedles referred to as 1-strand, 2-strand and 6-strand. These needles have different lengths of plastic gauge (tubing) which need to be moved on and off to alter the pile depth *(see Pile Depth on page 16)*.

The second set (No. 2 in the photograph) has a single handle with three different sized needle tips: small, medium and large. The spring-loaded action within the handle alters the pile depth.

THREADERS

Threaders are fine, specially-adapted looped wires for threading punchneedles. All punchneedles will be threaded in a similar manner. Threaders have two loops, the larger of which the thread is passed through. The thread is then gently pulled through the smaller loop to hold it in place while the threader is being pulled through the bore of the needle.

Types of threaders

There are two types of threaders *(see equipment photograph on page 6)*:
Type 1 (No. 3 in the photograph) is very fine and short with a pointed end and a looped end.
Type 2 (No. 4 in the photograph) is long and has a looped end. The point on this type is covered by a small square of paper *(see Threading the Punchneedle on page 19)*.

Threaders are quite fragile and easily broken, and therefore they require gentle use. Without a threader it is impossible to thread a punchneedle. They are an integral part of the threading process and can be easily lost, so find a container in which to safely store them.

GAUGES

Punchneedles use either a piece of plastic tube for a gauge or a built-in, spring-loaded, gauge regulator to alter the pile depth *(see Pile Depth on page 16)*.

FABRIC

A tightly woven fabric is required for punchneedle embroidery. Punchneedles can be very damaging to fabric and considerable care in the choice of fabric is necessary.

Detail from Crazy Angel Fish,
page 76.

Tip: Test a sample of fabric before starting on a project. Place the chosen fabric in a hoop and work some stitches with the punch-needle and thread which you intend to use. Undo the trial stitching and have a good look at the fabric to see if it is damaged. If you are able to coax the warp and weft back into place and the fibres have not been damaged, then that is a good indicator that the fabric is suitable. On the other hand, if the fabric is visibly damaged, consider using an iron-on interfacing on the back of the fabric.

There are many beautiful fabrics to choose from and often it is only through experimenting that you will find which fabric works more successfully than others.

Punchneedles work well on calico; however, be aware that there is a vast range in the quality of this fabric.

Pre-washing of fabric is a personal choice. If a finished item is likely to be washed (such as a piece of clothing), pre-wash it before embroidering. The 'sizing', or stiffening, in fabrics does not appear to damage the punchneedles.

Stretch fabrics, such as material for sweat shirts, require iron-on woven interfacing to be bonded to the back of the fabric prior to working. Alternatively, choose the applique method I describe (*see Applique of a Design on page 27*), which is ideal for this type of fabric. This eliminates the need to actually work on the stretch fabric.

The applique method is also an option for use with thick woollen blanketing, which is difficult to get tight in a hoop due to its bulkiness. Wool flannel is easier to manage as an alternative to blanketing.

IRON-ON INTERFACING

Iron-on interfacing is a soft, voile-like fabric with a special coating on the back which melts when heated and bonds to the back of another fabric. If you have chosen to work on a fabric which is too fine and fragile in nature for your selected punchneedle, you will have to consider using an iron-on interfacing. Use a *woven* interfacing as it is the weave of the fabric which holds the worked loops in place. Before ironing the interfacing into place, check that there is no fluff or hair between the interfacing and fabric; these can show up noticeably through some fabrics and spoil the look of a finished piece of work. Make sure the two layers are firmly bonded together.

HOOPS

When embroidering with punchneedles, it is important to have the fabric stretched as tightly as possible in a hoop. I have found it is best to use a plastic hoop which has an inner ring with a lip and outer ring with a handscrew for tightening. When this inner lip locks into place over the outer hoop, the fabric can be held securely and very tightly (drum-tight), which is the optimum for punchneedle embroidery.

The smaller the hoop size, the tighter the fabric can be pulled without too much effort. It is preferable to use a 10 cm (4"), or 15 cm (6") hoop; however, they restrict the size of a project. If you choose to use a 20 cm (8") or 25 cm (10") plastic hoop, be aware that tightness is essential.

THREADS

There is an incredible range of threads available, and the beauty of punchneedle embroidery means that we can work a huge variety of these threads into our creations. We can add life, colour, texture and richness to our embroideries and make two-dimensional work three-dimensional *(see figure 3 on page 33 and figure 10 on page 40)*. The colours, types, thickness and textures of thread are exciting. As long as the thread we choose can be easily threaded and can flow smoothly, we can use any thread available with our punchneedles.

The thread used is determined by the bore size of the punchneedle. We can use only one strand of thread or up to six strands of thread, 2 mm to 4 mm silk ribbon and other forms of ribbon which we can thread through the needles. Also fine wool, crochet cotton, and machine embroidery threads can be used. The only limitation is that the thread must flow through the needle smoothly and evenly.

With my designs, if I suggest a particular thread but it does not flow through your punchneedle smoothly, change to a thread that does. This may mean that you have to amend the drawing of a design by enlarging or reducing it.

For the projects in this book I have used Madeira thread and Appleton's wools. I enjoy working with them as the quality is

Tip: Unless the fabric is drum-tight, punchneedle embroidery stitches will not stay in place. This is one of the main frustrations for a beginner embroiderer. Working with fabric which is not pulled tightly can cause a great deal of wrist stress as well, which can prove painful over time.

excellent, and there is a huge range and they are readily available. *(most craft suppliers carry a wide range of threads, but also consult a conversion chart if the recommended threads are not readily available in your area.)* I use different types of punchneedles for different projects and I know that some threads work well in some needles and not in others. For example, Madeira Decor thread, which gives a most interesting look to the punched loops, tends to shred a little due to the sharpness of some of my punchneedles. I then have to use a different punchneedle or find an alternative thread.

Punchneedle embroidery uses a lot of thread. Check before you start a project that you have sufficient of each colour. Work with the longest length of thread that you can manage, or work directly from a spool.

I cannot be absolutely specific about which threads will suit you or your needles. Have fun experimenting with your punchneedles and getting to know their capabilities. You will undoubtedly be pleasantly surprised.

MADEIRA MAGIC PEN

This is a double-ended felt tip marker. One end has a very fine point and the other has a thicker tip. The mark made by this pen can be removed with a damp cloth. These pens are great for marking the front of the fabric when working reverse punchneedle embroidery, as any mark not covered by embroidery can easily be removed.

IRON-ON TRANSFER PENCIL

Iron-on transfer pencils are another easy way of transferring a design onto fabric. The design is traced onto tracing paper, then positioned tracing-side down onto the fabric and ironed over with the iron set at an appropriate heat for the fabric. The drawn design becomes imprinted onto the fabric. The image you trace onto the paper is ironed onto the back of the fabric in reverse. The embroidery on the front of the fabric will face the same way as the initial tracing.

DRESSMAKER'S CARBON

Good quality dressmaker's carbon paper works a treat and is by far the simplest method of transferring a design onto the back of fabric.

It is best not to use it on the front of the work as it can be messy.

SCISSORS

Small, sharp embroidery scissors are essential. A pair of angled (slant-and-snip) scissors is ideal to cut out applique shapes.

TWEEZERS

Tweezers are invaluable when working reverse punchneedle embroidery. They are used to pull the beginning and ending threads through to the back of the fabric.

RULER

A small ruler is needed to measure pile depth.

CROCHET HOOK

Keep a very fine 0.75 crochet hook in your work kit. It is useful for pulling any long loops or ends that show up on the front of your work through to the back. Avoid cutting these threads on the front of the work as they tend to change colour when cut, leaving dark marks which show up dramatically on the finished work (*see figure 3 on page 33*). Use the crochet hook to pull unruly loops through to the back. Be extremely careful as it is easy to get the hook caught, thereby pulling out too many stitches. When retracting the crochet hook, do so in a gentle, twisting manner.

RAZOR BLADE

A sharp razor blade is helpful for cutting plastic gauges to the length required. Fine scissors can be used, but a razor blade gives a straighter cut. Place the plastic gauge onto a flat surface, then gently press the razor blade through the plastic to cut a straight edge.

PATTERNS AND DESIGNS

Wherever you look you will find ideas that will work well in punchneedle embroidery. Children's books, wrapping paper and cards are some sources of inspiration, or preferably draw your own original designs. Always be aware of copyright laws regarding the use of other artists' work.

When you have worked a few items you will begin to understand more about choosing designs for punchneedle embroidery. Take note of the designs which I have drawn. Simple is best! Remove detail, and reduce lines to a minimum. Another point to remember is that, on completion, the finished piece is often larger than the traced design. This is due to the thickness of the thread and the density of the punched loops *(see figure 2 on page 32)*. Where I have drawn a small design to be worked with a very fine needle and one strand of thread, you can choose to enlarge the design and work with a bigger needle and more strands of thread.

'YOU CAN WASH IT' CRAFT GLUE

This craft glue dries clear and remains flexible when smeared onto the back of punchneedle embroidery.

It is used to seal the edges of work in preparation for applique *(see Applique of a Design on page 27)* or for holding loops in place.

'OFF 'N ON' GLUE

'Off 'n On' glue is pressure-sensitive. It is applied to the back of a design and left to dry until it is tacky to touch. The design is then pressed onto a garment where it remains secure until removed. The tackiness lasts for a number of uses before the glue needs to be renewed. Using this product gives great versatility to a cut-out design which you would rather not have adhered permanently *(see Applique of a Design on page 27)*.

PUNCHNEEDLE EMBROIDERY

This is my first book on punchneedle embroidery, and the first published in Australia on this subject. It contains extra information not covered in this book along with many exciting and elegant designs. Published by The Five Mile Press, 1997.

E-mail me at *dndesign@eisa.net.au*

Techniques

TRANSFERRING THE DESIGN

There are many ways to transfer a design onto fabric, and you probably have a favourite method. I find that a light box is invaluable, but as not everyone has one of these there are other methods, such as using the light through a window. Below is one easy method to transfer a design.

1 Use a sharp lead pencil to give a very fine line. Wipe the sharpened end of the pencil with a tissue prior to use to prevent granules of carbon falling onto your work.
2 Trace the design onto tracing paper.
3 Turn the tracing over, so that it is reversed.
4 Tape the tracing of the design to a well-lit window.
5 Place the fabric over the tracing with the back of the fabric facing up.
6 Tape the fabric over the design and trace the design onto the back of the fabric.
7 To get an image onto the front of the fabric in preparation for reverse punchneedle embroidery, turn the fabric over, hold it up to a window and trace any required outline onto the front of the fabric.
8 When tracing onto the fabric only use a sharp lead pencil if it will be covered up by embroidery; alternatively, use the Madeira Magic pen. An iron-on transfer pencil and dressmaker's carbon paper are other options.

PLACING THE FABRIC IN THE HOOP

1 With the lip uppermost, place the inner ring flat on a table.
2 With the design facing upwards, spread the fabric over the inner hoop.
3 Loosen the screw on the outer ring and place this ring over the fabric on the inner ring. Press down until the outer ring locks into place under the lip of the inner ring. Then tighten the screw.
4 Turn the hoop over, placing the fabric flat upon the table. With your fingers inside the hoop and your thumbs outside, work round the hoop, pulling the fabric extremely tight. Check that the design is not distorted and that the warp and weft of the fabric remain straight. Tighten the screw and keep repeating this process until the fabric is taut.

Tip: One of the few reasons that loops will not stay in place is because the fabric is not tight enough in the hoop.

Tip: to remove dirty marks made when tightening the screw on the hoop, take a clean handkerchief or face cloth, wrap it around the index finger, moisten it with water and softly rub it across a bar of soap. Gently rub the offending mark, then move the cloth around to a clean spot. Moisten it again and wipe away any soap. Remove any marks before pressing as heat will set them.

Having the fabric stretched very tightly in the hoop opens the warp and weft of the fabric. (The warp goes up and down and the weft goes from 'weft to wite' — that is, left to right.) The tighter the fabric, the easier it is for the needle to find its way between the threads. At this point, when the fabric is stretched tightly in the hoop, if a loop is pulled the work can easily come undone. When the fabric is removed from the hoop, the fibres relax and tighten around the loops, holding them securely in place. This is the reason knotting or tying to start or finish the stitching is not required. (*Also see What Keeps the Loops in Place on page 23.*)

If the design you are working on is larger than the hoop size, you will need to move the hoop and place it over previously embroidered work. When the hoop is removed the stitching may be flattened. Usually this will not damage the work, but if it does you need to consider the quality of thread that is being used. The flattened area can be fluffed up by scratching on the pile with your fingernail, or holding a steam iron over the affected area.

There is one drawback to using plastic hoops in which the fabric is pulled drum tight. Frequently the hoop leaves a circular mark that is difficult to remove from the fabric. This mark can be removed by steaming with an iron or pressing with a chemically treated cloth, such as a Rajah cloth. To prevent the imprint to some extent, cut a circle of calico with the centre cut out like a doughnut (*see photograph on facing page 17*). This is then placed between the two rings of the hoop on the front of the fabric. The calico circle also protects the fabric from dirty marks generated from the natural oils of our fingers, especially where the screw is being constantly tightened and the thumb rubs upon the fabric (*see tip at left*).

PILE DEPTH

I refer to pile depth as the length of the loops made on the front of the fabric. A gauge is required to set the depth to which the needle can be inserted into the fabric and gives an evenness to the loops made. The needle tip will penetrate just as far as the needle handle or a gauge placed on the needle will allow.

The pile depth is measured from the eye of the needle to the end of the plastic tube, or to the bottom of the handle in some types of punchneedles.

Some punchneedles need a plastic tube to be cut to the appropriate length to give the pile depth required. These tubes can be made from the insulation surrounding small gauge (new and unused) electrical wire after removing the wire. Soak the plastic tube in some warm water to soften it if it is too tight to easily slip onto the needle. Alternatively, the plastic tube may be too loose, in which case thread a piece of thread through the tube to give a tighter fit when slipped onto the needle.

The built-in gauge on other types of punchneedles makes the altering of the length of loops very simple. The lowest setting on this type of punchneedle is 10 mm (No 1). This length can be too long for some work. If this is the case, place a small piece of plastic tube onto the needle to get a shorter loop.

The length of the loop formed on the front of the fabric is half of the measurement of the pile depth. For example, a measured 10 mm pile depth gives a loop length of 5 mm. Some length of the loop will be taken up by the thickness of the fabric. Allow for the thickness and fluffy nature of some fabrics when measuring pile depth.

Tip: If the gauge is too long it will result in a very short loop which will not be long enough to stay in place. Shorten the length of the plastic tube.

When working on a number of different projects at the same time it is easy to forget the pile depth you are working with. Keep a record by writing the measurement on the outside of the fabric being used.

The two different types of punchneedles I prefer to work with have different methods of setting pile depth: Type 1 *(No. 1 in the photograph on page 6)* is altered by placing a plastic tube onto the needle. Type 2 *(No. 2 in the photograph on page 6)* can be altered by the spring-loaded action in the handle. A regulator showing No 1 to No12 is marked on the handle.

AN APPROXIMATE CONVERSION CHART

Type 1	Type 2
6 mm & 8mm	Measure a piece of plastic tube as for Type 1 (6 mm can be too short for some of these needles)
10 mm	No 1
12 mm	No 2
14 mm	No 3
15 mm	No 4
16 mm	No 5
18 mm	No 7
20 mm	No 8
25 mm	No 10
28 mm	No 12

The conversion chart shows the millimetre measurement for the Type 1 punchneedle compared to the numerical setting for the Type 2. *(See the photograph on page 6: Type 1 is marked with a 1, and Type 2 is marked with a 2.)* The conversion chart is approximate only as differences in the length of the needle may vary.

Use this printed ruler as a guide for measuring.

MARKING THE STRAIGHT GRAIN ONTO FABRIC

Use the crochet hook when you need to mark the straight grain on fabric. Place the fabric in the hoop and tighten it. Place the back of the hook onto the fabric between two rows of weave. Press upon this and drag it firmly between the rows. This separates the rows slightly and leaves a mark which is easy to see and work along. This line may look crooked when the fabric is stretched in the hoop. It straightens when the fabric is removed from the hoop.

CARE OF PUNCHNEEDLES

The needle tips of punchneedles are fragile and they require care to prevent damage or burring from dropping or stabbing into harsh objects. A burr can be gently filed away with a fine emery board used for fingernails or very fine sandpaper. Some punchneedles have a spring-loaded action which enables the needle tip to be retracted and housed safely. Others come with plastic sheaths in which the needle tip is placed when not in use.

THREADING THE PUNCHNEEDLE

1 The threader is inserted from the eye end of the punchneedle, through the hollow of the needle and handle, until the looped end protrudes from the handle.

2 At the looped end of the threader, the thread is pulled into the small loop which holds it securely.

3 Take the end of the threader which protrudes from the eye end of the punchneedle and pull it through the hollow of the needle and handle until the thread, which is held in the small loop, appears at the end of the needle.

4 The thread is then threaded through the eye of the needle making this a two-part process, quite different from threading an ordinary sewing needle. Depending on the type of threader

Tip: It is important to remember that it is a two-part process to thread the punchneedle, and often one reason a punchneedle is not working properly is because the thread has only been passed down the shaft and not through the eye of the punchneedle as well.

being used *(see Types of Threaders on page 9)*, the following will occur:

(a) The threader described as Type 1 remains threaded and sufficient thread is pulled out from the shaft of the needle to allow the threader to be turned around. The pointed end is then inserted through the eye of the needle from the bevelled side. Then the thread is pulled gently through the eye, and the thread gently removed from the fragile threader.

(b) The threader described as Type 2 has the thread unthreaded from it at this stage. The loop of the threader is inserted from the straight side of the needle, through the eye. The thread which has been pulled through the bore of the needle and the handle is picked up and pulled into the small loop of the threader. The threader and thread are drawn back through the eye of the needle. Then the thread is removed from the threader.

STITCHING WITH YOUR PUNCHNEEDLES

1 Thread the punchneedle, then check the flow of the thread through the punchneedle.

2 Stretch the fabric tightly in the hoop. Hold the hoop in a comfortable position.

3 Have the bevelled edge of the punchneedle travelling in the direction you will be stitching. I am right-handed and choose to work with the bevelled edge of my needle facing out to the left, but still working towards me. You can also stitch with the bevelled edge working directly forward. The way you choose to hold the needle is a personal thing. Work in whatever manner you are most comfortable with so long as you achieve the desired result. A straight appearance to the stitches is made with the bevelled edge of the needle travelling directly forward. A slanted stitch resembling stem stitch occurs with the bevelled edge of the needle facing outward *(see Special Effects on page 31)*.

4 Hold the punchneedle with your thumb, index and middle finger (like a pen). Rest the side of your hand and your little finger on the stretched fabric in the hoop *(see photograph on page 21)*.

5 Hold the punchneedle at right angles or at a little less than right angles to the fabric, whichever is the more comfortable for you.

6 It does not matter where you start stitching on a design.

7 Punch the needle through the fabric as far as the plastic gauge or handle on your punchneedle will allow. Withdraw the punchneedle until the tip is just skimming the surface of the fabric. Drag the needle along the surface of the fabric for a very short distance and punch the needle into the fabric again. The motion for working becomes lift-slide-punch into the fabric, lift-slide-punch into the fabric, and so on.

8 Turn your work over to check your progress. If your stitches are close enough together, they will make a continuous line of loops on the front of your work. If there are big gaps in the line of the loops, practise working the stitches closer. The next row of loops will fill in small spaces between the loops of the previous row.

9 You can let the end of the thread run right through the needle. Keep an eye on the thread as it flows through as it can knot up inside the handle and will be difficult to remove.

10 If there are many separate areas to be filled in with one particular colour, simply finish stitching in one area by holding the thread in place. This prevents any loops from coming undone. Pull the punchneedle along the thread far enough to start working elsewhere. When you have finished stitching, trim the long loop which has been formed on the back. Keep the back of your work tidy and free of long ends and loops as these loops can be easily pulled out.

11 Choose the manner which suits you to fill in your design. Maybe work a row of stitching around the outside edge of the area of a design and then fill in from the outside to the centre. When working in large areas, which can become monotonous, section off small areas and fill in piece by piece. You can stitch in any direction so long as you are holding your punchneedle with the bevelled edge travelling in the way you are working. I prefer to work with the needle travelling towards me, with the bevelled

Holding the punchneedle.

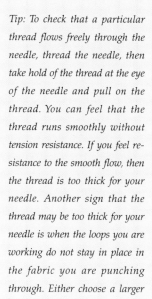

Tip: To check that a particular thread flows freely through the needle, thread the needle, then take hold of the thread at the eye of the needle and pull on the thread. You can feel that the thread runs smoothly without tension resistance. If you feel resistance to the smooth flow, then the thread is too thick for your needle. Another sign that the thread may be too thick for your needle is when the loops you are working do not stay in place in the fabric you are punching through. Either choose a larger needle or a finer thread.

Tip: If you lift the needle away from the fabric instead of merely skimming the surface, the loop already made underneath can be pulled out. If the punchneedle is turned around in your fingers and you begin to work in the direction of the eye of the needle, you will be working directly into the thread and the sharp point of the needle will cut the thread.

Practising the technique will find you mastering this versatile form of embroidery which can also add much dimension to traditional embroidery. Although it is a relatively easy form of embroidery, let that not detract from the potential to create beautiful and exciting pieces.

edge facing out to the left. I constantly turn my hoop rather than work backwards.

13 Check the front of your work, and you will soon have a good idea of spacing. The distance between the stitches is short and the distance between the rows is barely a punchneedle width. When the finished piece is held up to the light, gaps and areas of backing fabric may still be seen. Fill them in with some more stitching.

14 Take care that the needle does not push into the previous row of stitching, thereby pushing out loops already formed on the front. When this happens and a longer loop forms on the front, gently pull the loop through to the back with the crochet hook.

15 If the fabric becomes less than taut, use gentle pressure with your fingers to push up from under the hoop or down from the top of the fabric with your thumb to create more tension on the fabric.

Note: There are some sets of punchneedles that have a needle with a very fine bore and which can be threaded with one strand of thread.

If your smallest punchneedles suits two or three strands of thread and you wish to use only one strand, then try it. It is likely that the thread will slip through the needle too quickly, forming a loop where you are working.

You can correct this by putting some tension on the thread with your fingers as it enters the handle of the punchneedle, thereby keeping tension on the thread as it flows through the needle. If this is difficult to manage, work with two strands of thread for any design which suggests one strand of thread. The finished stitching will not be quite so fine.

CUTTING THREADS

Pull any finished ends to the back of the fabric before cutting them. You can cut threads on the front of the work, but be aware that some threads change colour when cut and can show up noticeably as a very different colour *(see Special Effects on page 31)*. This can spoil a completed piece of embroidery

When you need to finish a thread, hold it in place with your index finger at the point of exit to prevent it pulling out *(see photograph, top right)*. Slide the needle along the thread for a little way and either punch the needle into the fabric for safe-keeping or place it down securely to prevent it rolling. Cut the thread, leaving a short tag *(see photograph lower right)*.

When the thread runs out and leaves a tag on the front of your work, you can coax it through to the back by stroking it from behind with your fingernail until the end pops through, or carefully pull it through to the back with a crochet hook.

There will be times when loops are pushed out, causing them to become longer on the front than they are meant to be. Refrain from cutting these because of the manner in which some threads change colour when cut *(see figure 3 on page 33)*. Carefully pull them through to the back with a crochet hook.

WHAT KEEPS THE LOOPS IN PLACE?

Woven fabric has a warp and a weft, that is, the weave. When the fabric is stretched tightly in the hoop, the weave is opened, allowing the needle to slip easily into the spaces between the threads of the woven fabric.

When the embroidery on the design is complete, the piece is removed from the hoop, the tension is released and the fibres relax around the loops, thus holding them in place. This eliminates the need to do any over-sewing or knotting of the thread to begin or end off.

Nearly all the threads suitable for using in punchneedle embroidery have been spun and twisted. During the process of punching through

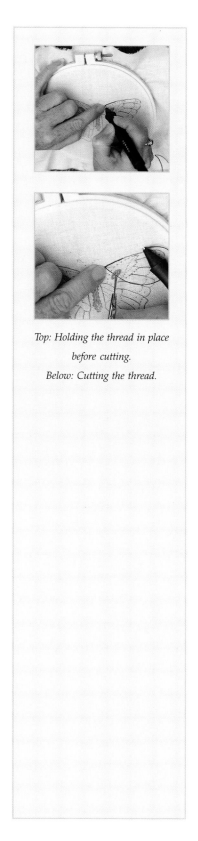

Top: Holding the thread in place before cutting.
Below: Cutting the thread.

the fabric and withdrawing the needle, a loop is left behind. If you turn your work over and look at this process in action you will see that the loop appears to twist upon itself and opens out, thus becoming bigger than the hole through which it was punched. With the relaxed weave hugging the loop, you can understand why the work does not readily pull out.

Do not re-use thread, as it tends to lose its twist; however if you are running short of thread and need to do this, be aware that it can give a different look to the formed loops.

The fabric and thread shrinks and matts a little when the completed piece is washed or dunked into warm water, thus enhancing the stability of the formed loops.

POSTURE

Be aware of how and where you are sitting when embroidering with your punchneedle. If you sit incorrectly, a lot of unnecessary strain is placed on your shoulders, arms and wrists. I have found that if I have my forearms and the hoop supported on a table as I work, this reduces stress and strain.

PROBLEMS? SOLUTIONS:

If the loops of your punchneedle embroidery will not stay in place or are not forming correctly, consider the following:

1   Is the needle threaded correctly? Remember it is a two-part process to thread the needle. First, the thread is passed through the hollow of the needle, and second it is threaded through the eye of the needle.

2   Is the thread caught on something, stopping it flowing freely through the needle? Or are you inadvertently holding the thread, preventing it from flowing through the needle?

3   Are you pulling the needle too far out of the fabric before sliding onto the next stitch, thereby not allowing a loop to be formed?

4   Is there a knot on the thread inside the handle of the punchneedle? Be very careful about trying to tug the thread down into the shaft of the punchneedle. It is extremely difficult, if not impossible, to get a blockage out of some of the fine needles. Thankfully some types of punchneedles can be screwed apart and any complication freed. The only way to dislodge anything 'stuck' inside the needle is to poke and prod and pray! Be very careful about scratching the inside of the needle whilst trying to dislodge anything. I have successfully burnt out a blockage from the stainless steel and brass needles by holding the blocked area over a candle. The heat chars the thread caught inside the needle and it can then be removed by passing a threaded threader through it; this has not affected the needle, but obviously it needs to be done with care.

5   If the pile depth is not long enough, the loops formed will be too short and will not stay in the fabric. Shorten the plastic gauge to make the loops longer.

6   Are you are using the wrong type of thread for the needle and the fabric, or unsuitable fabric for the needle and thread?

7   If the fabric is not in the hoop tightly enough, it is difficult for the loops to be formed.

8 Is the bevelled edge of the needle facing the wrong direction, causing it to cut and shred the thread?

9 If you are working the stitches too far apart, the thread which forms the loop will be taken up on the back of the work as a straight stitch and will not be long enough to stay in place.

10 The loops may not stay in place if, after removing earlier stitching, the threads in the fabric have not been coaxed back into place. Sometimes, the removal of stitches may damage the fabric and leave a hole. If this occurs, try the remedies suggested below:

How to repair a hole made in the fabric:

It can be very distressing when a hole is made in the fabric, especially when a great deal of work has already been done.

Depending on the situation here are a few suggestions:

• With an ordinary sewing needle threaded with one strand of matching thread, darn some threads into place and re-punch through these.

• Remove the work from the hoop, take a small piece of iron-on woven interfacing and with the point of a hot iron press into place with sufficient heat to bond it.

• With an ordinary sewing needle and matching thread, make some loops the same height, push them through the damaged fibres and fix into place with a smear of glue.

• If you do not have iron-on interfacing, glue a small fragment of fabric over the hole. Allow this to dry before re-punching some loops into it.

APPLIQUE OF A DESIGN

I often work designs on to calico, cut them out and then re-attach them elsewhere. I have done this for several projects in this book: the fish, seagull, a couple of the poinsettias and the teddy bear.

The method I use is to work the design and then remove the fabric from the hoop. Glue over the back of the completed piece with 'You Can Wash It' craft glue and about 6 mm onto the calico itself. Allow it to dry.

Carefully cut out the design close to the base of the outside row of stitching, using a small, sharp pair of slant scissors. Take care not to cut any loops; however, if you do, simply put a little bit of glue onto a pin tip and press this onto the cut loop and push it back into place.

In some projects, such as the petals on the poinsettia and the beak on the seagull, the points, when they are cut, may not look well-defined. Put a little glue between the thumb and index finger and press the fingers on to the sides of the pointed areas to sharpen them.

When the fabric has been cut, the white edge may detract from the finished item. Working on a coloured fabric similar to the colour of the outside row of stitching obviates this small problem.

Alternatively, as I prefer to work on calico, I paint the outside edge to match before cutting and then touch up the areas which have not taken the paint. I use water colour pencils, a matching coloured felt tip pen or fabric paints. I use whichever method is best-suited to the fabric or the colour I want.

The embroidered cut-out can be permanently attached with 'You Can Wash It' craft glue or by using 'Off 'N On' glue if it is not re-quired to be attached permanently.

This method of applique is ideal if you want to embellish a stretch-knit sweat shirt or woollen blanketing. I particularly like to applique these cut-outs as they give extra dimension to the look of a finished piece of work.

Detail from Crazy Night (page 53). A touch of glue has been used to hold the reverse punchneedle embroidery in place.

TO GLUE OR NOT TO GLUE?

Traditionally punchneedle embroidery was designed to be worked with the loops close together. When worked in this manner, the embroidery will hold securely in place and can be safely washed.

I work a lot of my designs in reverse punchneedle embroidery where the loops are more widely spaced. From what I have gleaned, as there is very little written on this form of embroidery, I believe it was never intended to be worked in this way. Working in this extended way by being more open in your work does not cause a problem. That is, until the question of washing or using it in a utilitarian manner such as a cushion or a quilt throw arises. This brings me to the question of using glue. I know that traditional embroiderers will throw their hands up with shock and horror at the mere thought of glue on the back of embroideries and I appreciate their concerns.

It is a dilemma that has concerned me for years. I have some knowledge of conservation, as I restored antique porcelain for many years. I am thus acutely aware of the associated concerns with glues, their properties, the process of aging and other inherent problems, such as the yellowing with age and how such products will react to fibres in the cloth being used.

Can you see the concerns? So what to do?

The decision to put glue onto your embroideries which can be damaging many years hence will have to be yours alone. If you are aware of this problem and have a concern, choose designs that do not place you in this dilemma.

I do not glue on any work which will be framed. It is when I work on items which will be used (for example, cushions), or the designs for my crazy patchwork pieces that the glue issue arises.

I use glue sparingly and am acutely aware that years down the track it may affect the fabric and threads. For now I am prepared to accept that it may be damaging as I continue to be totally fascinated with the way that punchneedle embroidery can be extended by working with the open effect which I have devised.

CHOOSING THE SIZE OF FABRIC FOR YOUR WORK

The fabric needs to be large enough to fit into the hoop with sufficient extra width to allow it to be pulled tight in the hoop.

As it is necessary to frequently turn the work over to check the progress, working with a large piece of fabric can be a nuisance. Often the fabric gets into all sorts of trouble, catching onto things, knocking things onto the floor and simply getting in the way. If it is necessary to work with a large piece of fabric, roll the edges and secure with safety pins to make working easier and safer.

WASHING

Punchneedle embroidery was traditionally designed to be worked with the loops close together such as in the teddy bear *(see Bear in a Crazy Patch on page 64)*. Worked in this manner, this form of embroidery washes well and actually improves with washing. A little care is required to ensure the piece does not come into contact with velcro or sharp fasteners which may catch on the loops.

Many of my pieces incorporate reverse punchneedle embroidery *(see Special Effects on page 31)* which is not densely punched, and the stitching is not close together. Careful washing of these pieces is necessary as the stitching may begin to come undone. If I know I will be washing work with reverse punchneedle embroidery on it, I will sparingly smear the back with You Can Wash It Craft Glue, which remains soft and pliable.

PRESSING

I choose not to iron over my embroidery. If you have to, place the embroidery face down on to a thick, fluffy towel and press into the pile of the towel. Alternatively, use a steam iron in the same manner as working with velvet, holding the iron above the piece and allowing the steam to raise up the pile.

It is sometimes necessary to steam press the fabric around the actual embroidery to remove the mark left by the hoop. Take special care if you are ironing calico which has not been pre-washed as it is notorious for scorching.

Tip: If you have a special piece of fabric which is too small to fit into the hoop, stitch calico borders onto it to make it large enough for your hoop (see photographs above)

Detail from Crazy with Fragrance, page 58.

Embroidery Guide

SPECIAL EFFECTS

There are numerous ways that punchneedle embroidery can be employed. The embroidery samples on the following pages illustrate a variety of ideas that show how versatile working with punchneedles can be. After a little practice you will be able to use your punchneedles adeptly to create stitches which will add depth, texture and character to your embroidery. You can also add variety to traditional embroidery by incorporating punchneedle embroidery.

NORMAL PUNCHNEEDLE EMBROIDERY

When I say normal punchneedle embroidery I mean the standard way that one works with punchneedles. That is, with a design printed onto the back of the fabric which is then embroidered with small running stitches, forming loops on the front.

There are many ways that this simple stitch can be worked. Short loops, long loops, loops which can be cut and sculpted and short and long loops combined (for example, in a flower to add dimension to a piece of embroidery).

Figure 1   *Figure 2*

Figure 1: Sample 1 (top) shows the stitching which is worked on the back of the fabric. Sample 2 (bottom) shows how the stitching of sample 1 looks on the front of the fabric. Three strands of thread have been used with a pile depth of 10 mm (No 1).

For the samples shown in *figure 2*, the box drawn at the top of the fabric is the same size as that which has been used to work the samples underneath.

The samples have been worked with three strands of thread at varying pile depth. From the top, 8 mm pile depth, through 10 mm, 12 mm, 14 mm, 16 mm and 20 mm pile depth.

Notice how much larger each sample becomes by increasing the pile depth, thereby increasing the length of the loops (*see Patterns and Designs on page 13 and 14*).

The photograph in *figure 3* shows samples of the various effects which can be achieved by cutting the loops of punchneedle embroidery. Samples have all been worked the same size using three strands of thread. It is easier to cut loops with the fabric removed from the hoop.

Sample 1 (from top): Loops worked with pile depth 20 mm.

Sample 2: Each loop has been cut individually at the very top.

Sample 3: The rounded part of the loops at the top has been cut off. This gives quite a different look to that of the sample above.

Sample 4: The loops have been cut low and straight across giving the lush velvet appearance. Notice also the marked change of colour, from that in the top sample, although the same thread has been used *(see Cutting Threads on page 23)*.

Sample 5: These loops have been sculpted. To do this remove the fabric from the hoop. Hold the fabric over the index finger and cut, leaving the top longer than the sides and outside edge thus giving a lovely rounded curve.

Figure 3

Figure 4 illustrates working around in a circle. Six strands of thread have been used.

Sample 1 (from top): This shows the stitching from the back. Initially when you start, the needle is punched into the fabric and a short tag of thread remains. Work closely around the tag, moving it out of the way as you work the first circle. Twenty stitches have been worked around the circle in this illustration. Use more or less stitches to achieve the size circle (flower) you want. *Sample 2* shows the front of the previous sample. This illustrates how to form a basic little flower which can have additional rows added to form a larger flower. In *sample 3*, the flower form has been worked with the method above but extra rounds have been added, altering the pile depth in each new round from 8 mm to 14 mm. Note the mark of the black line on the first sample —. This indicates where to change the pile depth when beginning a new round. In *sample 4*, the dome shape was started in the centre at 15 mm (No 4) pile depth, which was reduced to 8 mm at the outside edge.

Figure 4

REVERSE PUNCHNEEDLE EMBROIDERY

A fine, straight, running stitch is made on the back of the fabric in punchneedle embroidery. When worked on the front of the fabric, this stitch becomes an interesting surface stitch, adding a different look to the way punchneedle embroidery has long been known. I find it fascinating that, depending on the way the needle is held whilst working this stitch, many different effects are achieved from the one simple stitch.

Before working any reverse punchneedle embroidery, it is necessary to transfer that part of the pattern onto the front of your fabric so that you can use it as a guide. Hold the fabric up to a light source, and use your preferred method to transfer the pattern as required.

When working reverse punchneedle embroidery, it is also necessary to pull the beginning and ending threads through to the other side of the fabric. When starting to stitch, the beginning thread remains on the front of the fabric. Punch the needle into the fabric, hold it in place and turn the hoop over. Pull the beginning thread through from the front of the fabric to the back with the tweezers. When the area being worked is finished, hold the needle in place, turn the hoop over and pull the thread through the hollow of the punchneedle with the tweezers. Cut the thread, and withdraw the needle, leaving the thread at the back.

When stitching reverse punchneedle embroidery, you have more control when the area to be worked is uppermost in the hoop. If only a little section is to be worked in reverse punch, this can be done without removing the fabric from the hoop. Although it can be difficult to manage, you can turn the fabric over and work within the hollow of the hoop. In some of the designs on the pattern sheet, reverse punchneedle embroidery is indicated as such ----. For others, the instructions will specify where it is to be worked.

Upon completion of a piece of work where a lot of reverse punchneedle embroidery has been stitched, place padding at the back, to allow the loops to nestle into it. If padding is not used underneath, and the piece of embroidery is stretched into a frame, the loops are pushed up and cause a bulge.

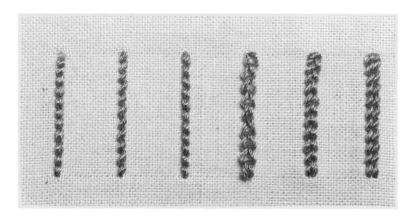

Figure 5

Figure 5 shows how various stitches can be achieved depending on how the needle is positioned while embroidering.

Sample 1: A straight stitch is formed when the bevelled edge of the needle is worked directly forward.

Sample 2: A beautiful stem stitch is formed when the needle is held with the bevelled edge facing out to the left whilst working directly forward.

Sample 3: A more raised stem stitch is formed when the needle is held with the bevelled edge facing outward, but this time working backward.

Sample 4: A chain stitch is formed when the eye of the needle travels backward. The thread is split and the needle is punched between the split threads. Increase the pile depth as some of it is taken up with the length of the stitch.

Sample 5: A braid-like stitch is achieved by initially working a row directly forward as in *sample 2* and then working very close to this row, backwards, as in *sample 3.*

Sample 6: A rope effect is achieved by working a row as in *sample 2.* Cut the thread and, commencing at the top again, work another row the same, very close to the first.

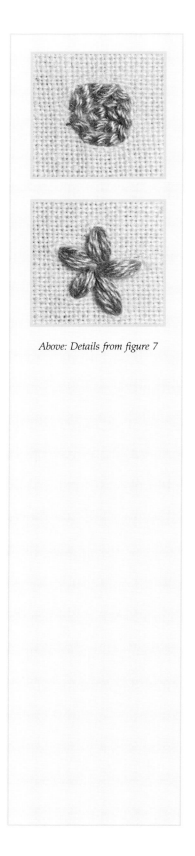

Above: Details from figure 7

COUNTING STITCHES

In various projects I indicate the number of stitches to work. They are counted like this:

- Punch the needle into the fabric. Do not count this as a stitch (although it does form a loop on the other side).

- Punch the needle into the fabric again and count the first straight stitch made as number one.

- Continue punching and counting as many stitches as required. For example, ten stitches counted will produce eleven loops (*see figure 6*).

- The number of stitches indicated in my designs are a guide only. Individuals work in different ways and to achieve the desired result may need to work more or less stitches.

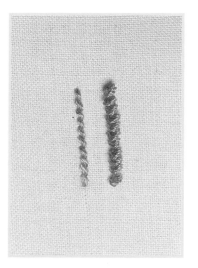

Figure 6

Figure 7

The photograph in *figure 7* shows various ways to use reverse punchneedle embroidery.

Sample 1: A small flower worked in reverse punchneedle embroidery in the same manner as *figure 4, sample 1 (see page 33),* with the ends pulled through to the back..

Sample 2: A star shaped flower worked with a pile depth of 15 mm (No 4). Work with a longer pile depth to accommodate the length taken up by the stitches. Commence in the centre. Punch a stitch in the centre, then out to the desired length, and then back to the centre. Work around the flower in this way. To achieve a thicker appearance to each petal work twice into the same holes.

Sample 3: A fine bud (or leaf). Work six stitches backwards as in *figure 5, sample 3 (page 35)* and then five stitches forward as in figure *5, sample 2 (page 35).*

Sample 4: A stem with leaves. Begin at the top. Work two stitches for the stem, work two stitches to the left at an upward angle, then return to the centre working two stitches alongside them.

Work two stitches to the right in the same manner, returning to the centre. Work two stitches for the stem and then continue like this for the length required. Use any number of stitches to vary the length of the leaf.

Tip: If the recommended threads are unavailable, experiment with other available threads or use a conversion chart to find a substitute.

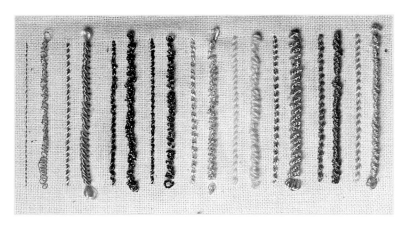

Figure 8

This photograph in *figure 8* shows some of the various Madeira threads which work well through punchneedles.

Sample 1: Machine embroidery thread works well in a 1-strand punchneedle. The reverse of this gives an extremely fine stitch suitable for working fine stems and for signing your name on finished work. My favourites are the variegated threads which come in a huge selection of colours.

Sample 2: Madeira Decor is a rayon thread used with overlockers. The colour range, sheen and effect achieved with it are stunning. It is not a twisted thread. It is made up with only one strand and gives an unusual but interesting look to the formed loop.

Sample 3: Madeira Glamour is a metallic thread with great sparkle which can add 'zing' to your work. A 'must have' for your workbox is No 2400. This has a pearlescent look which I favour for wings on insects *(see the insects in Bear In A Crazy Patch on page 64).*

Sample 4: Madeira Metallic thread No 5 comes in a variety of colours. This thread does not shred as readily as many gold metallic threads and works particularly well for reverse punchneedle embroidery *(see the gold basket in Crazy About Christmas on page 64).* It can be pulled apart and used as a single thread.

Sample 5: Madeira Metallic thread No 3010 comes in a variety of colours. A single strand of the rust colour has been used for the dragonfly with the teddy bear *(see Bear in a Crazy Patch on page 64).*

Sample 6: Candlewicking thread is available in lovely pastel colours as well as the usual ecru *(see A Paler Shade of Crazy on page 48).*

Sample 7: Madeira Decora has a beautiful lustre. It is made up of four strands which separate easily for finer work. Decora tends to curl upon itself and twists inside the punchneedles. Run a damp cloth along the length of the thread, which helps to keep it straight.

Sample 8: Madeira Silk comes in four strands which can be easily separated. For use in punchneedles, I equate four strands of Decora and Silk to six strands of Cotton should you need to replace one with the other.

Sample 9: Cotton has six strands and comes in a huge range of colours which harmonise within each colour group offering a shade for everything. They separate easily for finer work and glide beautifully through punchneedles to give a perfect finish.

Figure 9

Figure 9 shows additional threads and ribbons which, due to their thickness, give added texture when used in the larger punchneedles.

Sample 1: Ribbon Floss gives a glorious effect and comes in many colours.

Sample 2: 2 mm Silk Ribbon adds a different dimension to punchneedle embroidery.

Sample 3: Appleton's Crewel Wool comes in a huge range of colours. This fine wool works well on Wool Flannel *(see Crazy But Cozy on page 82).*

Sample 4: Appleton's Tapestry Wool flows well through the large punchneedle and works well on calico.

Sample 5: 4 mm Silk Ribbon flows well through the large punchneedle. The longer the loops the more stunning the effect.

Figure 10

The photograph in *figure 10* shows the formation of a flower.

Figure 10, sample 1: Work fourteen stitches around in a circle at 10 mm (No 1) pile depth.

Sample 2: Change the pile depth to 12 mm (No 2), work around the circle.

Sample 3: Change the pile depth to 14 mm (No 3), work around the circle.

Sample 4: Change the pile depth to 15 mm (No 4), work around the circle.

Sample 5: Change the pile depth to 16 mm (No 5), work this round.

Sample 6: Change the pile depth to 18 mm (No 7) for this round.

Sample 7: Change the pile depth to 20 mm (No 8) to work this round.

More rows and increased pile depth will form a bigger flower.

The photograph in *figure 11* below illustrates additional fill-in stitches.

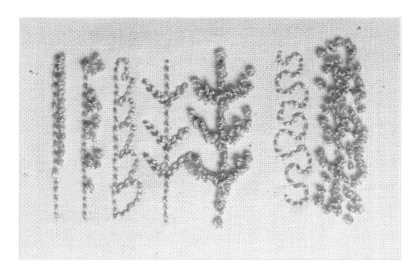

Figure 11

Figure 11, sample 1: A stem in reverse punch with loops along some part of it. It is ideal for grasses.

Sample 2: A stem in reverse punch with clusters of loops along it.

Sample 3: Decorative reverse punch, ideal for coral in an underwater seascape.

Sample 4: This is worked the same way as *sample 4* in *figure 7 (see page 36)* but with more stitches

Sample 5: Shows the other side of *sample 4.* A good way to work leaves.

Sample 6: Shows cornelli stitching. This is ideal for filling in background areas.

Sample 7: Shows the back of *sample 6.* This is a way to work spasmodic loops for filling in background areas.

Figure 12

Figure 12 illustrates different ways to work leaves.

Sample 1: This leaf is worked in reverse punch with the rows not too close together.

Sample 2: A leaf worked in the same manner as in *sample 1,* but showing the other side.

Sample 3 and *Sample 4:* These samples show other variations for working leaves.

Sample 5: Half of the leaf has been worked in reverse punch and the other half in normal punchneedle embroidery.

Sample 6: A leaf with the stitches worked closely in normal punchneedle embroidery.

Sample 7: The same leaf as in *sample 6;* however, in this sample a row of reverse punch has been worked close to the base of the loops. This makes the leaf look sharper and smaller.

Figure 13

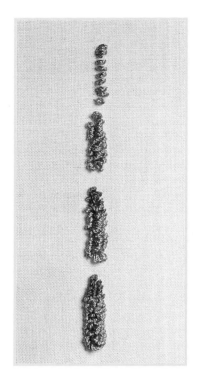

Figure 14

Figure 13 shows how to work a bud.

Sample 1: Work two rows of loops close together with a pile depth of 12 mm (No 2).

Sample 2: Change to 10 mm (No 1) pile depth to work a row around the first two rows.

Sample 3: Change to 8 mm pile depth to work another row.

Sample 4: A row of reverse punch has been worked close to the base of the loops.

The photograph in *figure 14* illustrates how to embroider lavender. The same principle is used to form petals for daisies without changing the colour for the tips.

Sample 1: Work a row with as many stitches as desired at 12 mm (No 2) pile depth.

Sample 2: Work around the former row at 10 mm pile depth.

Sample 3: Change colour. Work the tip in a V shape at 8 mm pile depth. Fill in the V.

Sample 4: Work around rows one and two in the same colour at 8 mm pile depth.

Detail from Crazy with Fragrance, page 59.

Detail from Crazy Angel Fish, page 76.

Crazy patchwork

Many wonderful books have been published showing various ways of putting together crazy patchwork. Please seek these out in libraries or bookstores or borrow them from friends. I discuss only very briefly the method for crazy patchwork as my aim has been to share with you my punchneedle embroidery techniques. I find crazy patchwork a wonderful canvas to work the magic of punchneedle embroidery upon, and an ideal way for me to put together two forms of needle art about which I am passionate.

Crazy patchwork, as the name implies, is patchwork put together in a crazy manner. There is no methodical way of piecing, but rather pieces of fabric are stitched together at random and attached to a base. In the past when I have worked crazy patchwork, I have used a soft fabric as my base fabric. Often when working punchneedle embroidery on crazy patchwork, the loops do not go all the way through the two layers but get lost in between. I now use a fine iron-on woven interfacing for the backing and bond this to the crazy patchwork.

In crazy patchwork many varied fabrics are used and there will be times when you want to use a fabric which is damaged easily by the punchneedle. Most fabrics can be used by having the iron-on interfacing fused to the back of them. My choice of fabric is usually determined by the colours I want to work with and, by having the added stability of the interfacing, very sheer fabrics can safely be used.

After each piece of fabric is stitched into place it needs to be ironed onto the interfacing. Make sure that the fabrics fuse together and that any small bubbles which form are pressed out. Extreme care needs to be taken to ensure that the hot iron does not come in contact with the adhesive on the back of the interfacing.

I piece my crazy patchwork before embroidering. When the finished patch is pulled tight in the hoop, the seams can come apart if the beginning and ending stitches have not been strengthened.

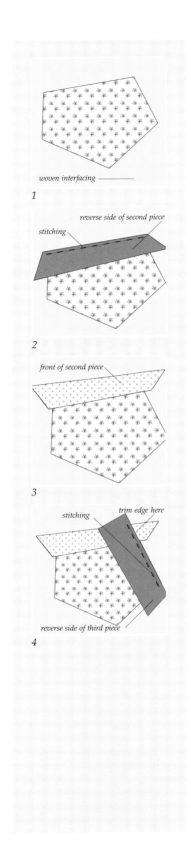

woven interfacing ————

1

reverse side of second piece

stitching

2

front of second piece

3

stitching   trim edge here

reverse side of third piece

4

Take care with the placement of designs near seams as it can be difficult to work through them.

Two projects in this book, the nightie and the teacosy, have not been patched, but simply had lines drawn onto the fabric which were then embroidered.

There are various ways of piecing crazy patchwork together. A number of years ago I was fortunate to be in a crazy patchwork class with Judith Montano, who wrote the wonderful book *The Crazy Quilt Handbook* (C & T Publishing). This is full of marvellous information on crazy patchwork and it is from there that I first learnt about punchneedle embroidery.

BASIC METHOD FOR MAKING A CRAZY PATCHWORK BLOCK

- Cut woven iron-on interfacing somewhat larger than the required size of the finished piece of work, then select fabrics in colours and textures of your choice.

- Choose the fabric for the centre piece and cut into a shape with five sides. Carefully iron it into place on the interfacing *(figure 1)*.

- Take the next choice of fabric and cut into an irregular shape. Make sure one of its edges is long enough to cover one edge of the original five-sided piece.

- Place this second piece of fabric upside-down on top of the five-sided piece (i.e. right side together). Align one edge with an edge of the five-sided piece below *(figure 2)*. Machine stitch a 6 mm seam, then flip the added piece over and press lightly onto the interfacing *(figure 3)*.

- Working in a clockwise direction, take the third choice of fabric. Check that it is long enough to cover the next edge of the five-sided piece, as well as the added second piece *(figure 4)*. In the same manner as above, machine stitch a 6 mm seam.

- Trim off any excess fabric beyond the seam *(figure 4)*, then flip the new piece over and press onto the interfacing *(figure 5)*.

- Take the next piece of fabric and attach it to the next edge of the five-sided central piece *(figures 6)*. Machine stitch a 6 mm seam, the flip, trim and press the piece into place *(figure 7)*.

Continue working in this manner until the required size is reached. Trim any edges and press the fabrics well to fuse the layers together.

EMBROIDERY FOR CRAZY PATCHWORK

My intention has been to show you how to extend the ways you use your punchneedles, and also to demonstrate how punchneedle embroidery and crazy patchwork can be worked together to great effect. I gain much of my enjoyment through decorating separate crazy patches with punchneedle embroidery.

On the following pages are nine projects which show how easy it is to create beautiful embroidery with your punchneedles. The projects and the accompanying pattern sheets are intended as guides only, and will help you to experiment and create your own unique designs. While I have provided basic instructions for creating a crazy patchwork block, there are of course many books and magazines specialising in traditional surface stitches, and from these you can learn the basic stitches to embellish the seams of your patchwork.

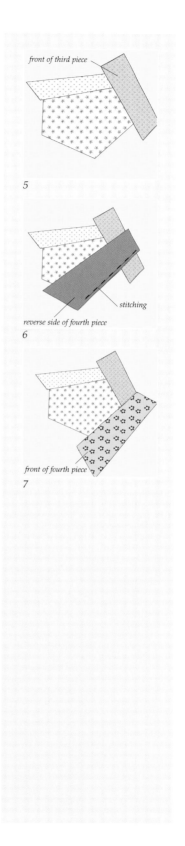

front of third piece

5

stitching

reverse side of fourth piece

6

front of fourth piece

7

Detail from Elegantly Crazy, page 70.

A Paler Shade of Crazy

This delicately toned, crazy-shaped heart is a delightful piece to work. It is intended simply to introduce you to the world of punchneedle embroidery.

Refer to the pattern sheet on page 89, and to Techniques and the Embroidery Guide on pages 15 and 31.

MATERIALS

- 20 cm (8") square fabric of your choice
- 20 cm (8") square iron-on woven interfacing (optional)
- 15 cm (6") plastic hoop with lip
- 3-strand or small punchneedle
- Candlewicking thread in colours pink, mauve, blue, green, lemon and ecru.
- Madeira Gold metallic No 9805, colour 5014.
- A selection of small pearl heart-shaped buttons, beads and sequins, and three small gold bees.

PREPARATION

1 Transfer the heart design onto the wrong side of the chosen, prepared fabric, using your preferred method of transferring.
2 Place work in hoop with the design facing upwards.

EMBROIDERY

1 Work at 8 mm pile depth for the whole design except for the pink heart.
2 Follow the colours given on the pattern sheet.
3 Change to 10 mm pile depth (No 1) to work the pink heart.
4 Work reverse punchneedle embroidery *(see Techniques on page 15)* around the inner and outer edges of the heart with the gold thread.
5 Stitch the small heart buttons, sequins and gold bees into place.

FINISHING

1 Press the fabric if necessary.
2 Choose a frame.
3 Place padding behind the embroidery before framing the finished piece.

Colour Me Crazy

This magically coloured cushion is rich and vibrant in colour and texture. It incorporates fourteen hearts and many techniques to illustrate the marvels of punchneedle embroidery.

Refer to the pattern sheet on page 89, and to Techniques and the Embroidery Guide on pages 15 and 31.

MATERIALS

- 30 cm (12") square fabric of your choice (plus extra for back and frill)
- 30 cm (12") square woven iron-on interfacing (optional)
- 6-strand or medium punchneedle .
- 20 cm (8") plastic hoop
- Madeira Decora, work with four strands

1556	*(rich blue)*	1479	*(emerald)*
1478	*(orange)*	1585	*(sea green)*
1470	*(old gold)*	1588	*(hot pink)*
1400	*(black)*		

- Madeira Stranded Cotton, work with six strands

903	*(purple)*	714	*(dark purple)*

- Madeira Metallic

    No 9805, colour 5017

PREPARATION

1 Transfer the heart design onto the wrong side of the chosen, prepared fabric, using your preferred method of transferring.
2 Place the fabric in the hoop with the design facing upwards.

EMBROIDERY

1 Work 10 mm (No 1) pile depth for the various colours indicated on the pattern sheet.
2 The deep purple velvet patch is worked in cotton 714, at 15 mm (No 4) pile depth.
3 Remove the work from the hoop and cut the loops to give the velvet look.

4 Replace the fabric into the hoop.

5 Work the black heart (between the emerald and purple) at 12 mm (No 2) pile depth.

6 Punch some gold loops randomly throughout this black area at 12 mm (No 2) pile depth.

7 The black heart within the orange area is not punched, allowing the colour of the base fabric to show through.

8 Work the small hot-pink velvet heart at 15 mm (No 4) pile depth and trim to give the velvet look.

9 Fill in the area at the top of the heart with Cotton 903. To achieve a rippled effect, work with one row of normal punchneedle embroidery, turn the hoop over and work two rows of reverse punchneedle embroidery. Continue in this manner to fill in the area indicated.

FINISHING

1 Make a gold braid with four thicknesses of gold metallic 5017, using twice the length of thread as the finished length required or use a fine purchased braid. Alternatively, with gold metallic 5017, work two rows of reverse punchneedle embroidery close together, around the inner and outer edges.

2 Stitch the braid around the inner and outer edges.

3 Make the finished crazy heart design into a cushion with a frill.

Crazy Night

Innocence and purity evoked from the simple stitch of the punchneedle. Choose a nightie pattern with a yoke which is suitable for crazy patchwork and embroidery. The patches on the yoke have not been pieced together but made to look like crazy patchwork by drawing lines for the seams which are then embroidered.

Refer to the pattern sheet on page 90, and to Techniques and the Embroidery Guide on pages 15 and 31.

MATERIALS

- Pattern and fabric of your choice
- Iron-on woven interfacing (optional)
- 3-strand or small punchneedle
- 15 cm (6") hoop
- 15 cms (6") of ribbon for the bow on the lavender
- Madeira Stranded Cotton

1701	*(pale green)*	102	*(lemon)*
801	*(mauve)*	502	*(pink)*
1002	*(pale blue)*	2401	*(white)*

- Mill Hill frosted glass beads 60161
- Madeira magic pen

Detail from Crazy Night (see photograph on page 55)

PREPARATION

1 Prepare the fabric. Iron on the interfacing if it is required.
2 Trace the outline of the yoke onto the chosen fabric.
3 Draw the lines for the seams with the marking pen.

EMBROIDERY

Three strands of thread have been used throughout for the hand embroidery and the punchneedle embroidery. Work with 8 mm pile depth for both the normal and the reverse punchneedle embroidery unless stated otherwise.

1 Hand embroider on the marked lines.
2 Trace the small designs onto each separate patch
3 Refer to the pattern sheet on page 90 for the stitching guide.

Bow

1 Use 801 for the bow. Fill in where indicated with normal punch.
2 The centre of the bow is worked by changing the pile depth to 15 mm (No 4).
3 Cut and sculpt the centre of the bow to give a gentle, rounded velvet look.
4 Outline the areas of normal punch with reverse punch, close to the base of the loops.

Flowers on a circle

1 Reverse punch the circle with white.
2 Reverse punch the entwining row with 1701.
3 Work a cluster of flowers with seven to ten loops in each flower. Use each of the colours, and intersperse the green throughout.
4 Randomly stitch some beads throughout the design.

Pink heart

1 Use 502 to fill in the heart shape.
2 Work a row of reverse punch, very close to the base of the loops on the inner and outer edges.

Lavender

Note: the drawing on the pattern sheet is a guide only.

Work the lavender flower from the centre to the outside edge.

1 Set the pile depth at 10 mm (No 1). Punch two rows of normal punch along the centre of the lavender flower *(see Special Effects on page 31).*

2 Work two rows on either side of the previous rows at 8 mm pile depth.

3 Work a row of reverse punch around the edges of the two lavender flowers, very close to the base of the loops.

4 Use 1701 to reverse punch the stem and leaves *(see Special Effects on page 31).* Starting from the base of the flowers work five or so stitches to begin the stem. Work five stitches out to the left at an upward angle then return to the stem working very close to the previous stitches. Work five stitches to the other side at an upward angle and then work back to the stem very close to the previous stitches. Work five or so stitches to form another part of the stem. Repeat this for as many leaves as required. Finish working the length of the stem.

5 Tie a bow around the stem.

Bluebirds

1 Use 1002 to reverse punch the outline of the birds.

2 Make a colonial or french knot for the eye

The initial

1 Draw your own initial and add some flourishes to it which can be worked in reverse punchneedle embroidery.

2 Work the main parts of the initial in normal punch with reverse punch close to the outside edges.

3 Work a few flowers and leaves into the design *(see Special Effects on page 31).*

4 Stitch a bead into the centre of each flower.

Butterfly

1 With 1002, reverse punch the outline and the antennae of the butterfly.

Rosebud

1 With 502, at 12 mm (No 2) pile depth, work the centre of the rose.

2 With 1701, at 12 mm (No 2), work one row around the pink bud.

3 Change the pile depth to 8 mm and work around the previous row with 1701.

4 Reverse punch around the outside edge of the rose with 1701.

5 Work two rows of reverse punch close together for the stems.

6 Work the sepals and the two leaves in reverse punch where indicated on the design.

7 Work the remaining leaves in normal punch, with reverse punch around the edges.

Dancing leaves

1 Use each of the six colours to work the six leaves dancing across the yoke.

2 Use the pattern sheet as a guide for stitching.

FINISHING

1 Trim and tidy up the threads on the back of the embroidery.

2 Lightly smear 'You Can Wash It' craft glue on to the back of the finished embroidery.

3 Add a lining to the yoke.

4 Make up the nightie in accordance with its instructions.

Crazy with Fragrance

The fragrance and richness of these beautiful punch-worked flowers will remain forever.

Refer to the pattern sheet on page 91, and to Techniques and the Embroidery Guide on pages 15 and 31.

MATERIALS

- Prepared crazy patchwork of your choice
- 40 cm (16") square fabric of your choice
- 40 cm (16") iron-on woven interfacing
- 6-strand or medium and large punchneedles
- 20 cm (8") hoop
- Madeira Stranded Cotton

808	*(pale pink)*	2610	*(light dusty pink)*
809	*(dusty pink)*	601	*(burgundy)*
810	*(brown-pink)*	1514	*(dark green)*
1602	*(mid green)*	1573	*(green)*
2101	*(cream)*		

- 4 mm silk ribbon, approximately 1 metre (39")
- 5 mm-7 mm sheer pink organza ribbon, approximately 1 metre (39")
- 4 mm rayon embroidery ribbon in rich burgundy and cream, approximately 1 metre (39") of each.

  Note: The last three ribbons mentioned will only work through the large punchneedle. 4mm and 7mm ribbons will not work in the 6 strand punchneedle. Choose a finer ribbon which will flow easily through this needle and work an increased number of loops.
- Gold bow

PREPARATION

1 Iron the iron-on woven interfacing onto the back of your chosen fabric.
2 Transfer the design onto the back of the fabric using your preferred method of transferring. Trace the stems onto the front, ready for the reverse punchneedle embroidery.

EMBROIDERY

Use six strands of thread throughout.

Bottom flower

row 1: Start with 10 mm (No 1) pile depth and 601, work fourteen stitches around in a circle.

row 2: Change to 12 mm (No 2) and 810, work fourteen stitches around the first circle.

row 3: Change to 15 mm (No 4) with 810, work around the previous circle.

row 4: Change to 16 mm (No 5) and 809 to work this round.

row 5: Change to 18 mm (No 7) with 809, work around the circle.

row 6: Change to 20 mm (No 8) and 2610, work around the circle.

row 7: Change to 25 mm (No 10) with 2610, work the final round.

Middle flower

row 1: Start with 10 mm (No 1) pile depth with 601, work fourteen stitches around in a circle.

row 2: Change to 12 mm (No 2) and 810, work fourteen stitches around in a circle.

row 3: Change to 14 mm (No 3) with 810, work around the circle.

row 4: Change to 15 mm (No 4) and 809, work around the circle.

row 5: Change to 16 mm (No 5) with 809, work this round.

row 6: Change to 18 mm (No 7) and 2610, work around the circle.

row 7: Change to 20 mm (No 8) with 2610, work around the circle.

row 8: Change to 25 mm (No 10) and 808, work the final round.

Three-quarter flower

row 1: Start with 10 mm (No 1) pile depth and 810, work eight stitches around in a circle.

row 2: Change to 14 mm (No 3) and 809, work only three-quarters of the way around the circle.

row 3: Repeat row 2.

row 4: Change to 15 mm (No 4) and 2610, work the three-quarters.

row 5: Change to 16 mm (No 5) with 2610, work the three-quarters.

row 6: Change to 18 mm (No 7) and 808, work three quarters.

row 7: Repeat row 6.

Greenery above bow

Work the bottom green near the bow at 25 mm (No 10), inter-mingling 1514 and 1602 where indicated on the pattern. Do not work this too densely.

Leaves

1 There are five leaves. Work the bottom three with 1602 at 8 mm (*see Pile Depth on page 16*).
2 The top two leaves are worked with 1513.
3 Turn the work over and carefully work a row of reverse punchneedle embroidery in the centre of each leaf to form a vein.

Buds

1 At pile depth 14 mm (No 3) and 809, work two rows of six stitches side by side.
2 Change to 12 mm (No 2), work one row around the previous two rows.
3 Change to 10 mm (No 1) and work one row around the previous rows.

Long skinny buds

1 Work three buds of each colour, 2101 and 601, with 8 mm pile depth. Work ten stitches first then nine stitches alongside them.

Organza Ribbon Flowers

1 There are five organza flowers. The two larger ones are worked at 28 mm (No 12) with five stitches in a circle.
2 The medium organza flower is worked at 25 mm (No 10) with eight stitches.
3 The smaller organza flowers are worked at 16 mm (No 5) with nine stitches in a circle.

Silk ribbon flowers

1 There are three silk flowers. The bottom two flowers are worked at 25 mm (No 10) with ten stitches in a circle.
2 The top flower is worked at 15 mm (No 4) with eighteen stitches.
3 Work a couple of areas in 1514 at 15 mm (No 4) with twenty stitches.

Add greenery sporadically throughout with 1602 at 10 mm (No 1).

Domed flower

1 Make a mark on the fabric so you can see where each round begins.
2 Start with 14 mm (No 3) and 601. Work ten stitches around in a circle. Work around this with 12 mm (No 2) and then finally around it with 10 mm (No 1).

Cream flowers

1 Begin with 14 mm (No 3) pile depth and 2101, work ten stitches around in a circle. Work around this at 10 mm (No 1).

Cream and burgundy rayon flowers

1 There are three of each colour. Work two burgundy and one cream at the bottom with a pile depth at 20 mm (No 8), with five stitches.
2 Work the remaining two cream flowers and one burgundy in the middle of the design at 15 mm (No 4), with five stitches.

Stems

1 Remove the fabric from the hoop, turn it over with the almost finished design uppermost. Work all of the green stems in reverse punch using a mixture of all of the greens.
2 The pale pink stems and buds are worked in reverse punch with 808.

FINISHING

Stitch the gold bow into place over the stems.

Make up as desired, either into a cushion or have the finished piece framed.

Bear in a Crazy Patch

Some people just 'sits and thinks'. I just 'sits and sits' in a crazy patch with my garden friends.

Refer to the pattern sheet on pages 91 and 92, and to Techniques and the Embroidery Guide on pages 15 and 31.

MATERIALS

Make up the background crazy patch, 25 cm (10") square, in the colours of your choice.

Materials for the insects

- 1-strand punchneedle
- 15 cm (6") hoop
- Madeira Silk

230	*(rust)*	1508	*(grey green)*

- Madeira Stranded Cotton

2003	*(dark brown)*	1513	*(green)*
2400	*(black)*		

- Madeira Glamour No 8, colour 2400 pearlescent
- Madeira machine embroidery thread, No 40, colour gold-3

The insects have been worked with a very fine punchneedle with one strand of thread (except where stated) at a pile depth of 6 mm (or 8 mm if you choose). With minor alterations it is possible to work these designs with a 3-strand or small punchneedle using two strands of thread. With the small punchneedle it may be necessary to work with a pile depth of 8 mm.

Materials for the bear

- 20 cm (8") square calico
- 15 cm (6") hoop
- 3-strand or small punchneedle
- Madeira Stranded Cotton

2103	*(mid tan)*	2102	*(pale tan)*
2105	*(dark tan)*	2003	*(dark brown)*
1513	*(green)*	1313	*(dark green)*
1311	*(mid green)*		

Detail of the twin ants from Bear in a Crazy Patch.

- Madeira Decora

1432	*(mauve)*	1517	*(pink)*
2401	*(white)*	1466	*(yellow)*

- a pair of 4 mm topaz eyes
- 'You Can Wash It' craft glue

PREPARATION

Note: the insects are worked in both reverse and normal punchneedle embroidery.

1 Transfer the designs onto the patches using your preferred method of transferring. Some parts of the designs will be on the back and the others on the front in preparation for the reverse punch.
2 Place the fabric in the hoop.

EMBROIDERY

I have used a couple of threads in this piece with which you may not be familiar. For the spider's web and the wings on the butterfly, bee and dragonfly, I have used one strand of Glamour No 8, colour 2400. Glamour is a metallic effect yarn, used for overlocking and decorative sewing on the sewing machine. It is made up of six thin strands, twisted into one. The strands separate easily and work well in punchneedles, either the whole six twists (making one strand) together, or separated out. Use one strand only for the wings.

The dragonfly has been worked with another metallic thread, No 9803, colour copper. It is made up of twelve very fine strands, twisted into one. Use two strands to work the dragonfly.

THE INSECTS

Hovering Bee
1 Work in reverse punch with 2003 for the stripes.
2 Use one strand of Glamour pearlescent for the wings and a colonial or french knot for the eyes.

Big-eyed fly
1 Work in reverse punch in the same colours as the bee but make big colonial knots for his eyes in 1513.

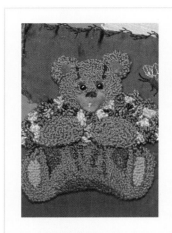

Detail from Bear in a Crazy Patch.

Cheeky cricket

1 Work the outline in reverse punch with 1513. Fill in the body with reverse punch. This fellow has gold colonial knots for his eyes and a colonial knot for his mouth in 1513.

Long skinny ant

1 Fill in the body parts with reverse punch. Finely work legs and antennae and add two small colonial knots in 2306 for his eyes.

Green caterpillar

1 Work the body in normal punch. Reverse punch around the entire body very close to the base of the loops. Work the legs and antennae in reverse punch.

The ant twins

1 Work in the same manner as the caterpillar but add colonial knots in 2306 for the eyes.

Gold-backed regal beetle

1 Work the outline, legs and antennae in 2003.
2 Fill in the back area with gold reverse punch.
3 Make a thick colonial knot in 2003. Add small gold colonial knots at the end of the antennae.

Lady-bird imposter

Not quite a lady-bird is she?
1 Work the body in normal punch with 2003 and 2306.
2 Work the legs and antennae in 2003.
3 Add colonial knots in 2306 at the end of the antennae.

Rusty beetle

1 Work with 2306 in the same manner as the ant twins, adding colonial knots in 2003 for the eyes.

Sumptuous spider

1 Work in the same manner as the ant twins, using 2306 in the marked section on his back.

Dragonfly

1 Work in reverse punch using two strands of copper for the filled in section of the body parts, the legs and antennae.

2 Fill in the wings with reverse punch, using one strand of Glamour pearlescent.

3 Add colonial knots in 2003 for the eyes.

Butterfly

1 Work the body in normal punch with 2306.

2 Work the outlines for the wings with one strand of Glamour pearlescent. The legs and antennae are worked in reverse punch with 2003.

Shining spider's web

1 Work in reverse punch using one strand of Madeira Glamour pearlescent.

2 Attach a long strand of thread from the web to the spider.

FINISHING

Frame the embroidered crazy patch square with padding behind it, ready for the bear to be attached.

The Bear

The bear is worked with three strands of thread throughout. Transfer the design onto the back of the calico and place the fabric into the hoop.

Head

1 Work the two lines marked on the head with 2003 at 8 mm pile depth.

2 Fill in the head area with 2103 at 8 mm, working around the eyes, nose and mouth area. Jump across the lines which have been worked in 2003 as you come to them.

3 Work the inner row near to the eyes at 10 mm (No 1).

4 Work the outer areas of the ears at 10 mm (No 1) with 2103.

5 Work the inner ear at 14 mm pile depth (No 3) with 2102.

6 Work the area around the mouth at 14 mm (No 3).

7 Remove the fabric from the hoop.

8 Cut the 14 mm loops of the inner ear and the mouth area. Shape and sculpt this area until you are happy with the effect.

Detail of dragonfly from Bear in a Crazy Patch.

Nose

1 See the diagram on page 91. Cut 50 cms (20") of 2003. Use the full six strands.

2 Fold the length into four. Tie a knot by wrapping the thread around twice. Work the knot into the centre of the thread.

3 At each side of the area marked for the nose, gently make a hole in the fabric with a crochet hook.

4 Pull an end of the 2003 thread through each made hole, from the front to the back.

5 Position the knot in place, on the front, for the nose. Tie the ends at the back to secure the knot in place.

Mouth

1 Thread a needle with four strands of 1517 and work a colonial knot for the mouth.

Eyes

1 The eyes which I use are plastic and have a plastic shank. Cut the shank off, flush with the back of the eye, with old scissors.

2 Put a small amount of glue onto the back of the eye and carefully position the eye into place. You need to gently push the remaining short length of shank through the fabric by gently working a small hole into the weave of the fabric without actually damaging the fibres. This allows the eye to sit flush with the fabric.

3 Allow to dry.

4 Replace the fabric into the hoop.

Note: If the cushion is to be used by a young child, do not use small plastic eyes. Instead, embroider the eyes using a suitable thread.

BODY

1 Work the arms at 12 mm (No 2) pile depth.

2 Work the area under the arms with a mixture of 1513,1313,1311 then stitch in the stems at 10 mm (No 1).

3 The remainder of the bear is worked at 8 mm pile depth. Follow the design on the pattern sheet for colour changes and shading.

4 Work one row of 2105 around the pad of the paw.

Flowers

1 Work the flower colours randomly, working in small circles of 8, 10 or 12 stitches at 12 mm (No 2) pile depth near the paws, changing to 10 mm (No 1) toward the face.

FINISHING

1 Remove the fabric from the hoop .

2 Glue over the back of the bear.

3 Allow to dry.

4 Cut the bear away from the calico.

5 Glue the bear into place onto the crazy patchwork square. Use the techniques described in *Applique of a Design* on page 27.

Detail of the teddy bear from Bear in a Crazy Patch

Elegantly Crazy

The stunning elegance of punchneedle embroidery captured and suspended in the colours of autumn.

Refer to the pattern sheet on page 93, and to Techniques and the Embroidery Guide on pages 15 and 31.

MATERIALS

- Prepared crazy patchwork fabric of your choice
- Finished size of the cushion (without the frill) is 37 cms (14½") square.
- Finished size of the diagonal strip is approximately 15 cms (6") x 50 cms (20").
- 1-strand punchneedle
- 10 cm (4") and 15 cm (6") hoop
- Madeira Decora

1482	*(cream)*	1528	*(pinky brown)*
1425	*(rich mustard)*	1542	*(darker shade of 1528)*
1470	*(old gold)*	1484	*(pinky cream)*
1558	*(rust)*	1549	*(pale old gold)*
1571	*(mustard)*	1526	*(dark caramel)*

- Madeira Silk

2213	*(mustard)*	2306	*(rust)*
1510	*(pale green)*	1508	*(dark green)*

- Madeira Metallic 9805, colour 5014
- Madeira Glamour No 8, colour 2400
- Assorted gold charms

PREPARATION

1 Make up the crazy patchwork strip and then sew very wide calico borders around it. This allows for easy movement of the hoop around the fabric while doing the embroidery.
2 Transfer the designs on to the fabric. Some of the designs or parts of the designs will need to be transferred to the front of the fabric for working the reverse punchneedle embroidery.
3 Place the fabric in the hoop.

Note: Use the pattern sheet on pages 92 and 93, which indicates stitches, threads and colours as a guide for each of the small designs. The reverse punchneedle embroidery is shown on the pattern sheet as

– – – – – – – – – – – – –

EMBROIDERY

The designs for this cushion have been worked with a very fine punchneedle, using one strand of thread at a pile depth of 6 mm, unless otherwise stated.

With minor alterations it will be possible to work these designs with a 3-strand or small punchneedle using two strands of thread. With the small punchneedle it may be necessary to work with a pile depth of 8 mm.

Bird and hill

1   The bird and background hill are worked in reverse punchneedle embroidery.
2   Use 1510 for the hill.
3   Use 1542 for the outline of the bird and then 1484 for the inside lines.
4   Make a colonial or french knot for the eye with 1425.

Three connecting leaves

1   Work with both normal and reverse punchneedle embroidery.
2   Use 2306 and 1508, then 1484, 1470 and 1571.
3   Work reverse punch around the outside edge of the normal punch, very close to the base of the last row of loops.

Rose bud

1   Work all of the design (except the sepals) in normal punchneedle embroidery with a row of reverse punchneedle embroidery around the outside edges.
2   Use 1508, 1510 and 2306 then 1425 and 1470
3   Work the leaves in 5108 and 1510, adding touches of 1470 and 2306.
4   Work two rows in 1508 for the stems.
5   Work the sepals with 1508 in reverse punch.

Butterfly

1 Work in normal punchneedle embroidery with a row of reverse punchneedle embroidery around the outside edge of each section.
2 Use 1470, 1482, 1425, 1549 and 1571.
3 Embroider the antennae and the small section of wing indicated on the pattern sheet with reverse punch.

Dragonfly

1 Work completely in reverse punchneedle embroidery.
2 Use 1508 and Glamour No 8, 2400 *(see explanation in Bear in a Crazy Patch, page 64),* which has a pearlescent look and is used for the fine stitching inside the wings.

Apples and pears

1 These are worked with both normal punchneedle embroidery and reverse punchneedle embroidery.
2 Add gold apple and pear charms. If you are unable to find these, embroider the apples and pears with normal punch in the colour of your choice.
3 Use 1425,1484, 1470, 1542 and 1482 then 1510, 1508 and 2306.
4 Reverse punch around each fully filled-in leaf.

Beetle on the leaves

1 Use 2306, 1510 and 1508 then 1484, 1470 and 1425
2 The leaves are all worked in reverse punchneedle embroidery.
3 Work the beetle in normal punch.
   Note: Start in the centre of the body with the pile depth at 8 mm, changing to 7 mm and then 6 mm as you work toward the outside edge. This gives a rounded appearance to the back.
4 Work the head the same as No 3.
5 Reverse punch around the body and head.
6 Carefully work a row of reverse punchneedle embroidery between the head and body to define the two areas.
7 Make colonial or French knots for the eyes.

Three Leaves on a stem

1   Use 1510 and 1508 then 1425 and 1558.
2   These leaves are worked with both normal punchneedle embroidery and reverse punchneedle embroidery as indicated on the pattern sheet.
3   The leaf to the left has three rows of normal punch along the far side.
4   The bottom leaf has one row of normal punch along the lower edge.
5   Work two rows of normal punch for the stem and base.
6   Reverse punch around all of the edges.

Caterpillar on a leaf

1   Use 2306, 1510 and 1508 then 1484, 1470 and 1425.
2   The leaf is worked in reverse punchneedle embroidery.
3   The caterpillar is worked in normal punch.
4   In the second and third section (marked 2 and 3 on the pattern sheet) of 1558, work 6 loops with a pile depth of 15 mm. Cut and shape these longer stitches to give a furry appearance.
5   Work a row of reverse punch around the caterpillar.

Garden

1   Work from the pattern sheet using normal punchneedle embroidery and reverse punchneedle embroidery where indicated.
2   Use 1508, 2213 and 1510 then 1482, 1484, 1542 and 1470
3   For the clusters of flowers, change the pile depth to 15 mm, work in a circle and make about twenty loops.
4   The flowers on the stems are worked with a pile depth of 10 mm.
5   Refer to the pattern sheet for embroidering the leaves. Shown there in detail are some varied appearances in which to work the reverse punch.
6   Add some gold leaf charms (optional).

Garden With Cobblestones

1 Use 1510 and 1508 then 1470, 1528, 1526, 1558 and 1542.

2 Work from the pattern sheet, using normal punchneedle embroidery and reverse punchneedle embroidery where indicated.

3 When working the scattered loops along the reverse punch grassy stems, work four or so loops very close together and then work four loops along the stem, and then another four close together. Repeat this to the end.

4 The star-shaped flowers are worked in reverse punch with a longer pile depth to accommodate the length of the stitch. The larger star flowers are worked with 10 mm pile depth, the smaller size flowers are worked with 8 mm pile depth. *(See how to work these in Special Effects on page 31.)*

5 Add a couple of gold charm flowers or work some flowers as described in the two gardens.

FINISHING

1 On completion of the embroidery, remove the fabric from the hoop.

2 Cut the crazy patchwork and embroidered strip to shape so it will fit the cushion.

3 Stitch the strip into place across the diagonal of the cushion.

4 Make a braid using four strands of all the colours plus the gold, or use a purchased braid.

5 Stitch the braid into place.

6 Make up the cushion with a lovely, wide frill.

Detail of punchneedle embroidery in Elegantly Crazy.

Crazy Angel Fish

The beauty, colour and texture of the underwater world is recreated by the magic of punchneedle embroidery. This is a piece where you can be free with your stitching. Put in your own personal touches, colours, and effects. The completed size is 30 cms x 30 cms (12"x 12"). Divide the work area into approximately one third each for the sky and sea. The embroidery takes up the final third.

Refer to the pattern sheet on page 94, and to Techniques and the Embroidery Guide on pages 15 and 31.

MATERIALS

- Fabric for the embroidery, approximately 30 cms x 50 cms (12" x 20"). You need it this size to be able to move the hoop around. Use a piece of fabric with a watery appearance or paint a piece of calico.
- Prepared crazy patchwork for the sky and sea, approximately 35 cms x 35 cms (14"x 14"). This size allows room for trimming when completed.
- Various sized punchneedles for the threads and ribbons you choose.
- 20 cm (8") or 25 cm (10") hoop
- Madeira Decor No 6

  1445 *(pale aqua)*   1447 *(pale green)*

  1514 *(pale pink)*
- Madeira Glamour No 8

  2458 *(emerald)*
- Madeira Rayon No 30

  2002 *(variegated)*
- Madeira Stranded Cotton

  903 *(purple)*   2705 *(dark sea green)*

  1003 *(blue)*   2502 *(burgundy)*

  1704 *(grey green)* 809 *(dusty pink)*
- 2 mm and 4 mm silk ribbon in pink, burgundy and blue
- Some found shells, assorted beads and charms
- Polymark bright gold glitter No PM 201 (This is a dimensional fabric and craft paint pen. The gold is suspended in clear glue and on application the glue dries clear and leaves a glittery gold behind)

Fish

- 20 cm (8") square calico for working the fish
- 3-strand or small punchneedle
- 15 cm (6") hoop
- Madeira Stranded Cotton, work with two strands

  2400   *(black)*   946   *(orange)*

  901   *(pale blue)*   106   *(yellow)*

  210   *(red)*

- Madeira Glamour 2400 pearlescent — separate and use three strands.
- Two small beads for the eyes
- 'You Can Wash It' craft glue

Seagull

- 20 cms (8") square calico
- 3-strand or small punchneedle
- 15 cm (6") hoop
- Madeira Stranded Cotton, work with two strands

  1813   *(grey)*

- Madeira Decora, work with two strands

  1471   *(white)*   1578   *(orange)*

- One small orange bead for the eye

PREPARATION

1 Transfer the design onto the back of your fabric, using your preferred method.

2 Hold the fabric up to a light source and draw in the areas worked in reverse punch needle embroidery onto the front of the fabric.

3 Place the fabric in the hoop. If the fabric size is too big to manage, roll and pin the edges.

EMBROIDERY FOR THE UNDERWATER SCENE

1 Punch along the base of the design using various threads and whichever punchneedle they flow through freely. The pile depth and number of strands of thread vary. Use a variety of pile depths from 10 mm to 25mm (No 1-No 10) and whatever number of strands in the punchneedles you choose to use. The aim is to put many different textures along the bottom and to have fun experimenting with your punchneedles. The areas which have the cut velvet appearance are worked at 20 mm-25 mm (No 8-No 10) pile depth and then cut.

2 Move the hoop whenever necessary

3 Some of the branching coral is worked in reverse punch needle embroidery and some worked from the back, leaving the loop on the front.

4 Work the silk ribbon in whichever needle it flows freely. Some needles are limited to using only 2 mm silk ribbon, so use this in place of the 4 mm, if necessary.

5 The 4 mm burgundy ribbon flowers are worked with a pile depth of 16 mm (No 5), working nine loops. A bead is then stitched in the middle and this helps to open out the loops to form a flower.

6 The blue silk clusters are worked in 2 mm silk ribbon, starting with 14 mm (No 3) pile depth at the base and changing through pile depths 12 mm (No. 2), 10 mm (No. 1) and 8 mm to the top.

7 The long variegated loops are worked at 20 mm to 25 mm (No 8-No 10) pile depth. The shell is then glued over the base of the loops which spreads the loops outwards.

8 The tiny pink flowers are worked at 10 mm (No 10) pile depth with seven loops and a small seed bead stitched into the centre.

9 Use the gold glitter glue to paint areas around the embroidery.

10 Stitch or glue in your choice of beads and charms.

11 Finally work two rows of stitching for the top edge. Use 2705 for the outside row and 1445 for the inner row at 10 mm pile depth.

12 Remove the fabric from the hoop.

Detail of fish and coral from Crazy Angel Fish

13 Glue the two top rows of loops with 'You Can Wash It' craft glue. Allow to dry before cutting out the shape along the outside row close to the base of the loops.

14 Stitch the finished embroidered base into place over the crazy patchwork foundation, at the side and base. Leave the top open.

EMBROIDERY FOR THE FISH

1 Transfer the fish outline onto the calico square using your preferred method.

2 Place the fabric into the hoop, with the design uppermost.

3 Work the black outline at 8 mm pile depth.

4 The area marked ::: is worked with two strands of Glamour 2400.

5 Fill in the stripes

6 Work the yellow circle for the eye and then stitch a bead into the centre.

7 Remove the work from the hoop.

8 Glue the back of the fish and allow to dry before cutting out (*see Applique of Design on page 27*).

9 Position and glue the fish into place over the completed crazy patchwork.

EMBROIDERY FOR THE SEAGULL

1 Transfer the seagull outline onto the calico square using your preferred method.

2 Place the fabric into the hoop, with the design uppermost.

3 Work the outlines in 1813 at 8 mm pile depth.

4 Fill in with 1471, leaving a space for sewing in the bead for the eye.

5 Stitch in the bead.

6 Glue the back of the seagull and allow to dry before cutting out.

7 Position and glue the seagull over the crazy patchwork.

Either make the completed picture into a wall hanging or have it framed.

Crazy but Cozy

A punchneedle adventure into the cosy warmth of wool embroidery.

Refer to the pattern sheet on page 95 and to Techniques and the Embroidery Guide on pages 15 and 31.

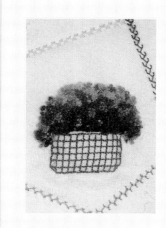

Detail from Crazy but Cosy.

MATERIALS

- Teacosy pattern of your choice
- 50 cm (20") square of wool flannel
- padding and lining fabric
- 6-strand or medium punchneedle
- 20 cm (8") hoop
- Appleton's Crewel Wool

  Nos: 101 *(pale mauve)* 102 *(light mauve)*

  103 *(mid mauve)* 104 *(dark mauve)*

  105 *(purple)* 106 *(deep purple)*

  352 *(pale green)* 163 *(very pale mauve)*

  354 *(light green)* 356 *(mid green)*

  358 *(dark green)* 552 *(yellow)*

  766 *(brown)*

- Madeira Magic pen

PREPARATION

1 Mark the shape of the tea cosy onto the flannel.

2 Draw the lines in a crazy manner with the Magic pen.

3 Hand embroider the marked lines to create imitated crazy patchwork. Then transfer the designs onto the back of the flannel.

4 Place the flannel into the hoop with the design uppermost.

EMBROIDERY

Basket

1 Transfer the image of the basket onto the front of the flannel.

2 Place the flannel in the hoop with the basket design uppermost.

3 Work the basket weave in reverse with 766 at 10 mm (No 1).

4 Pull all beginning and ending threads to the back. Trim the ends.

5 Remove the flannel from the hoop. Turn it over and put back into the hoop, ready to work the flowers

Flowers in the basket

1 Use 102, 103, 104, 105 and 163 for the flowers, using the basic flower (*see Special Effects on page 31*). For the greenery, use 354, 356 and 358.

2 Divide the floral area into three. In the bottom third work with the pile depth set at 12 mm (No 2), change to 10 mm (No 1) for the middle and use 8 mm for the top third. Intersperse all of the colours, using the darker colours at the base with the lighter colours toward the top.

3 Hold the flower basket upside down or up to a mirror. This gives a better indication of the effect of colour placement and overall balance.

Lavender

1 Use 101, 102, 103, 352, 354 and 356.

2 Use the strokes indicated for lavender on the pattern sheet as a guide.

3 With 101, work ten stitches at 12 mm (No 2) pile depth along the stroke.

4 Change to 102 and 10 mm (No 1). Work two rows on each side of the first row worked.

5 Change to 103 and 8 mm to work the lavender tips. Punch the needle into the fabric to continue the outside row in 102. Work in a V-shape with five stitches to the point and five more to the other outside row. Fill inside the V to form the tip.

6 Remove the flannel from the hoop and turn over. Replace into the hoop.

7 Work the stems in reverse punch using three greens, 352, 354 and 356.

8 Take a 20 cm (8") length of all the colours used plus 358 and tie a bow around the stems.

Pansy

1 Use 101, 102, 103, 104, 105, 106, 552, 766, 352, 356, and 358.

2 Work at 10 mm (No 1) pile depth.

3 Stitch the whiskers in the front and two side petals with 106.

4 Outline the front petal and the two back petals with 106.

5 Outline the two side petals in 105.

6 The whiskers in the two back petals are worked with 766.

7 In between all of the whiskers, work a row with 101.

8 Work the V in the centre with 552.

9 With 766, work five stitches in the centre of the yellow V.

10 Fill in the remaining areas of the front with 104.

11 Fill in the remaining areas of the side petals with 103.

12 Fill in the remaining parts of the back petals with 102.

13 Work the leaves by randomly incorporating 352, 356, and 358.

Daisy

1 The strokes for the daisy petals indicated on the pattern sheet are a guide only. Use 101, 102,104, 106, 163, 552, 356 and 358.

2 With 101 and 10 mm (No 1) pile depth, work nine stitches along the marked stroke for each petal.

3 Work with 102 along one side and then the other of the first row, forming a point at the tip of each petal.

4 Work around each petal with 104.

5 Work about eight stitches in the centre using 552 at 16 mm (No 5) pile depth. Add a few stitches into the centre with 106 and 163 to give an effect that pleases you.

6 The bud is worked with 104 at 10 mm (No 1).

7 Use both 356 and 358 to work the leaf at 10 mm (No 1).

8 Reverse punch the stems and under the bud with 358, working two rows of stitching close together.

Wisteria

1 Use 101, 102, 104, 105, 354, 356 and 766.

2   Stitch the bough with 766 at 10mm (No 1) pile depth.

3 The entwining stem and centre stalk of the wisteria blossom are worked in one row of reverse punch with 356. The crook-shaped stem is worked with two rows, close together, of reverse punch.

4 Work the leaves with 354 at 10mm (No 1).

5 The wisteria blossom is worked with 101, 102, 104, and 105 intermingled throughout. At the top of the blossom use 15 mm (No 4) pile depth. Graduate through varying depths from 15 mm (No 4) to 10 mm (No 1) to the tip.

FINISHING

1 The reverse punch used for the basket creates a concave effect. Cut a piece of padding the same size as the basket and glue into place over the back of the basket weave to push it forward.

2 Use a needle and 766 to work little running stitches close to and around the outside edge of the basket when the lining and padding are in place. Stitch through all of the layers to give the basket a padded effect.

3 Cut out and make up the tea cosy as desired.

4 Make a braid using all of the colours in the embroidery or use a purchased braid. Stitch the braid into place.

Crazy About Christmas

This spectacular gold basket holding a display of vibrant Christmas cheer is a tribute to the astonishing beauty of punchneedle embroidery. The front poinsettias are worked on separate fabric, cut out and placed on the basket to create depth and realism into the design.

Refer to the pattern sheet on page 95, and to Techniques and the Embroidery Guide on pages 15 and 31.

MATERIALS

- 40 cm (16") square tightly woven fabric
- 25 cm (10") square calico
- 40 cm (16") iron-on woven interfacing
- 3-strand or small punchneedle
- 6-strand or large punchneedle
- 20 cm (8") plastic hoop with lip
- Madeira Stranded Cotton (work with three strands)

      1313 *(dark green)*   2401 *(white)*
- Madeira Decora (work with two strands throughout)

      1570 *(dark green)*   1556 *(olive green)*
      1547 *(scarlet)*   1439 *(dark red)*
      1437 *(orange/red)*
- Madeira Gold No 5 colour 5012
- 4 mm white or cream rayon embroidery ribbon (or choose a ribbon which will flow freely through your largest punchneedle)
- Mill Hill seed beads No. 02013 (red)
- Nymo thread for sewing on the beads
- Needle for sewing on the beads
- 'You Can Wash It' craft glue

PREPARATION

1 Iron the interfacing onto the back of the fabric if necessary.
2 Trace the design onto the back of the fabric, placing the base of the basket 10 cm (4") from the bottom of the fabric.
3 Transfer the two front poinsettias and two front leaves of the design onto the calico as well.
4 Hold the fabric up to a light source and trace the basket onto the front, ready for working the reverse punchneedle embroidery.

EMBROIDERY

Basket

The basket is worked in reverse punchneedle embroidery.

1 Place the fabric into the hoop with the basket design uppermost. Protect the front with a calico doughnut *(see pages 16 and 17)*.

2 With Gold 5012 in the 3-strand or small punchneedle, at 10 mm (No 1) pile depth, work the lines of the basket as indicated on the pattern sheet, in reverse punchneedle embroidery. Fill in between the two bottom rows on the basket by working reverse punchneedle embroidery closely together

3 Pull all of the beginning and ending threads through to the back of the fabric *(refer to Reverse punchneedle embroidery in Techniques on page 34)*. Then trim all of the threads

4 Remove fabric from the hoop, turn the fabric over and replace into the hoop with the flower design uppermost.

Note: Trace the two front poinsettias and the two front leaves onto the calico. They are worked onto the calico, the edges are glued, allowed to dry, then they are cut out and placed into the basket.

The poinsettia

1 Work the two front poinsettias as indicated on the pattern sheet.

2 The under petals are shown as //// on the pattern sheet. Work the shadow, shown bold on the pattern sheet, on these petals with 1439 at 8 mm pile depth.

3 Work the veins, shown with a bold line, with 1439.

4 The rest of the under petals are filled with 1547 at 8 mm.

5 The petals shown ::: have the shadow and veins worked with 1439 at 10mm (No 1).

6 Fill in the petals shown ::: with one strand 1547 and one strand 1437 together through the punchneedle at 10 mm (No 1).

7 On the pattern sheet the upper petals have no shading. Work the veins on these petals with 1439 at 12 mm (No 2).

8 Fill in the remainder of the upper petals with 1437 at 12 mm (No 2) pile depth. Then fill in the centre of the flowers with white cotton at 10 mm (No 1) pile depth.

9 With 1556 work twenty or so stitches at 15 mm (No 4) carefully in a circle through the already worked white centre.

The two front leaves

1 These are worked onto the calico.

2 Fill in the leaves with 1556 at 10mm (No 1).

Remove the fabric from the hoop.

See *Applique of Design* on page 27 for the cutting and painting of the edges of the poinsettias and the leaves in preparation for placing into the basket. The cutting is important as this gives shape to the flower. If you want a sharper point to the petals, put a (very) little glue on your thumb and index finger tip, and press the sides of petal tips between the thumb and finger to form a point.

Attach the two poinsettias and two leaves where indicated on the pattern ·sheet. However, before doing so, randomly work some loops at 10 mm (No 1) where the pointsettias are to be placed. The loops will support the flowers and raise them up. The two leaves are attached under the poinsettias and over the basket.

The small poinsettia

This is worked in the same manner as the other poinsettias, however this poinsettia is worked directly onto the same fabric as the basket.

Detail from Crazy About Christmas. See full photograph on page 4..

Holly leaves, berries and stems.

Fill in with 1570 at 10mm (No 1). For the berries, work seven or so stitches in a circle at the base of each holly leaf with 1439 at 10mm (No. 1). Then work the stems with 1439 in reverse punch.

Remaining leaves

Fill in with 1556 at 8 mm pile depth.

Feathery leaves

1 Work these in reverse punchneedle embroidery with Cotton 1313.
2 Begin with two stitches to begin the stalk, which will have the feathery leaves attached.
3 Work four stitches out to the left and up at an angle.
4 Work back to the stalk with four stitches close to the previous row.
5 Work two stitches for the stalk
6 Work four stitches out to the other side in the same manner as 3.
7 As for No 4.
8 Continue in this manner for the full length.

Cream Flowers

1 Use your choice of ribbon which will flow easily through your punchneedle. These flowers are shown as circles with an 'x' on the pattern sheet. Work them at 15 mm pile depth.
2 Add some reverse punch stems to these little flowers with 1313.

Greenery

1 These are indicated by a small filled-in circle on the pattern sheet. Work a few stitches at 15 mm (No 4) with 1313.
2 With 1313 at 10 mm (No 1) work a few stitches intermittently throughout the design.

FINISHING

Remove the fabric from the hoop and trim the threads on the back. With Nymo thread, sew a red bead into the centre of each cream flower. Press the fabric well, being careful not to iron over the embroidery. Before placing the finished piece into the frame, place padding behind the embroidery into which the loops at the back of the basket can nestle. Frame the finished piece with your prepared crazy patchwork.

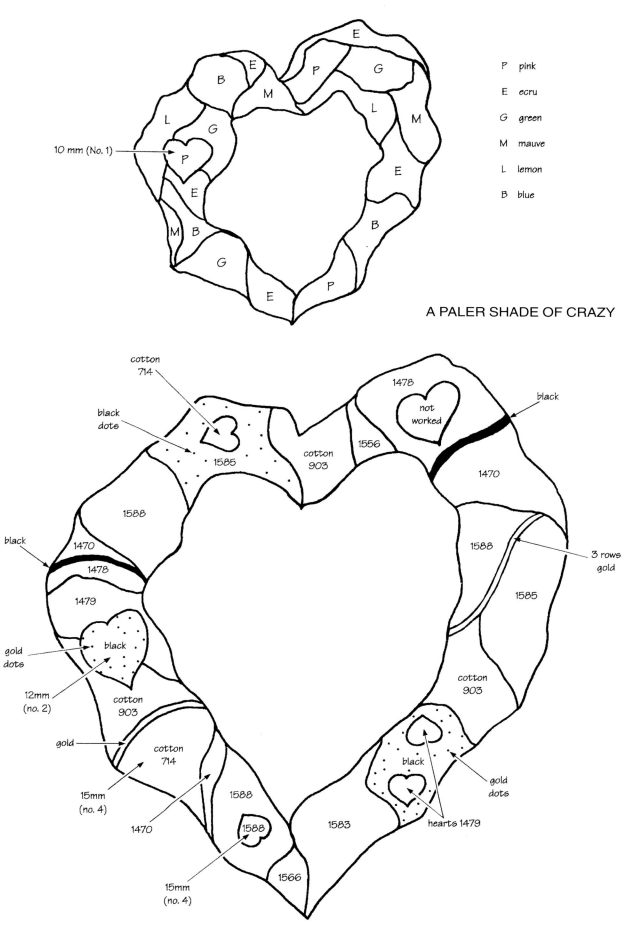

P pink

E ecru

G green

M mauve

L lemon

B blue

10 mm (No. 1)

A PALER SHADE OF CRAZY

cotton 714

black dots

1478

not worked

black

1556

cotton 903

1470

1585

1588

black

1470

1588

1478

3 rows gold

1479

1585

black

gold dots

black

12mm (no. 2)

cotton 903

cotton 903

gold

cotton 714

15mm (no. 4)

1470

1588

black

gold dots

1588

1583

hearts 1479

15mm (no. 4)

1566

COLOUR ME CRAZY

- - - - - - reverse punchneedle embroidery

———— normal punchneedle embroidery

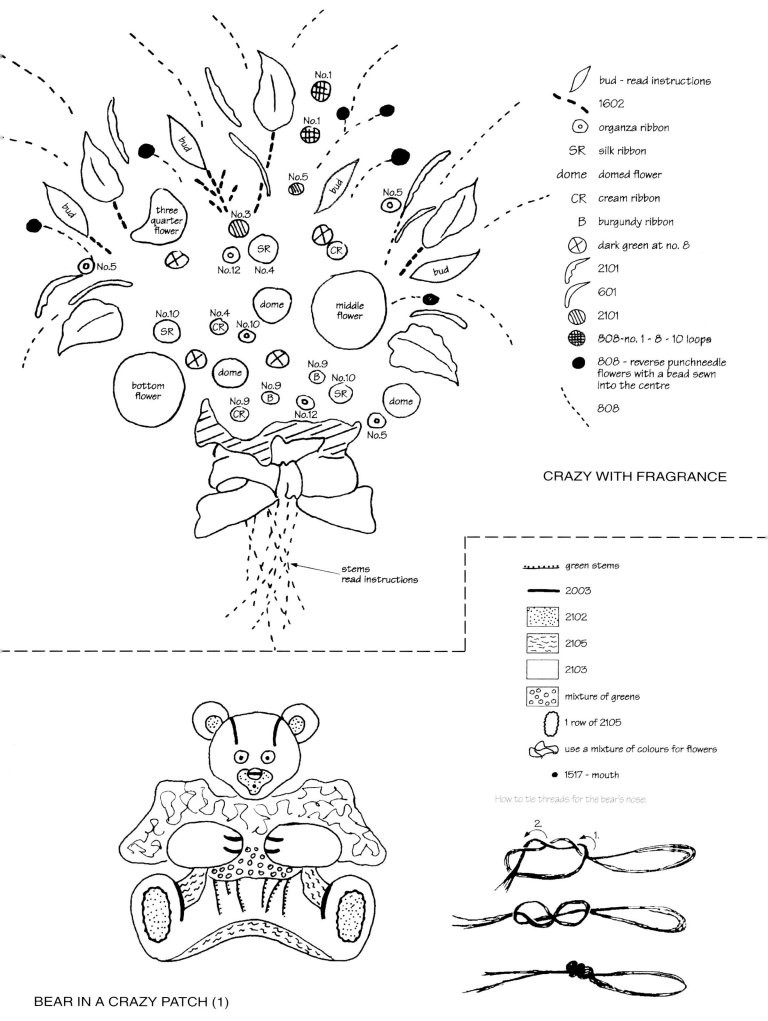

No.1

No.1

bud

No.5

bud

three
quarter
flower

No.3

No.5

bud

No.5

SR

CR

No.12   No.4

dome

middle
flower

No.10   No.4   No.10

SR   CR

bud

dome

No.9

bottom
flower

dome

No.9   B   No.10

B   SR

dome

No.9

CR   No.12

No.5

CRAZY WITH FRAGRANCE

stems
read instructions

bud - read instructions

1602

organza ribbon

SR   silk ribbon

dome   domed flower

CR   cream ribbon

B   burgundy ribbon

dark green at no. 8

2101

601

2101

808 - no. 1 - 8 - 10 loops

808 - reverse punchneedle
flowers with a bead sewn
into the centre

808

green stems

2003

2102

2105

2103

mixture of greens

1 row of 2105

use a mixture of colours for flowers

1517 - mouth

How to tie threads for the bear's nose:

2.   1.

BEAR IN A CRAZY PATCH (1)

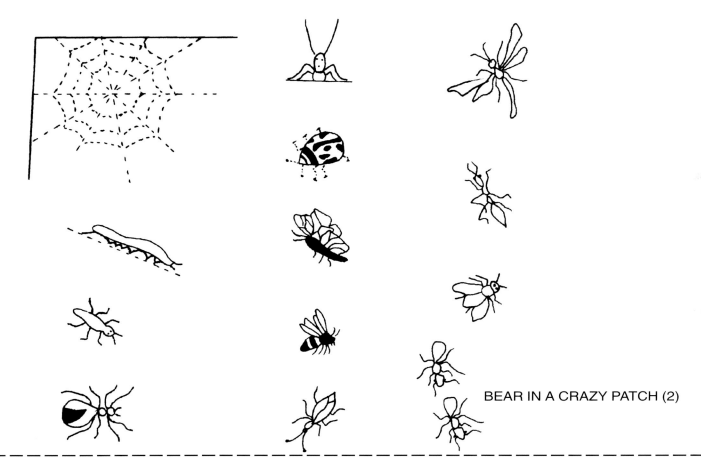

BEAR IN A CRAZY PATCH (2)

ELEGANTLY CRAZY (1)

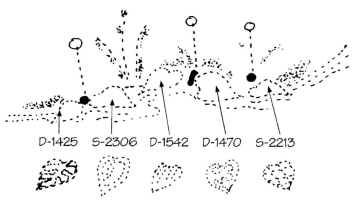

D-1425 S-2306 D-1542 D-1470 S-2213

○ D-1482 with pile depth at 10mm

- - - - mixture of S-1508
               D-1542

🐛 with S-1510 scatter some small
    areas of greenery in and around
    the design.

● cluster of 20 loops worked with
    pile depth at 15mm in:
               D-1484
               D-1470
               S-2213

mixture of: S-1510
               D-1470
work some scattered loops along
the seams.

mixture of small
scattered
loops of: S-1510
         D-1528

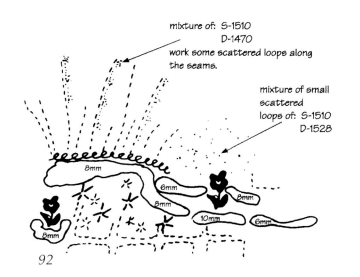

ℓℓℓℓℓ S-1508 at 6mm pile depth

⁘ D-1470 at pile depth of 8mm

✳ D-1542 at pile depth of 10mm

🌷 gold charm

● cobblestones D-1528

● areas marked 6,8,10mm work
    in various colours:
               D-1526
               D-1558
               D-1508
               D-1542
               D-1425

92

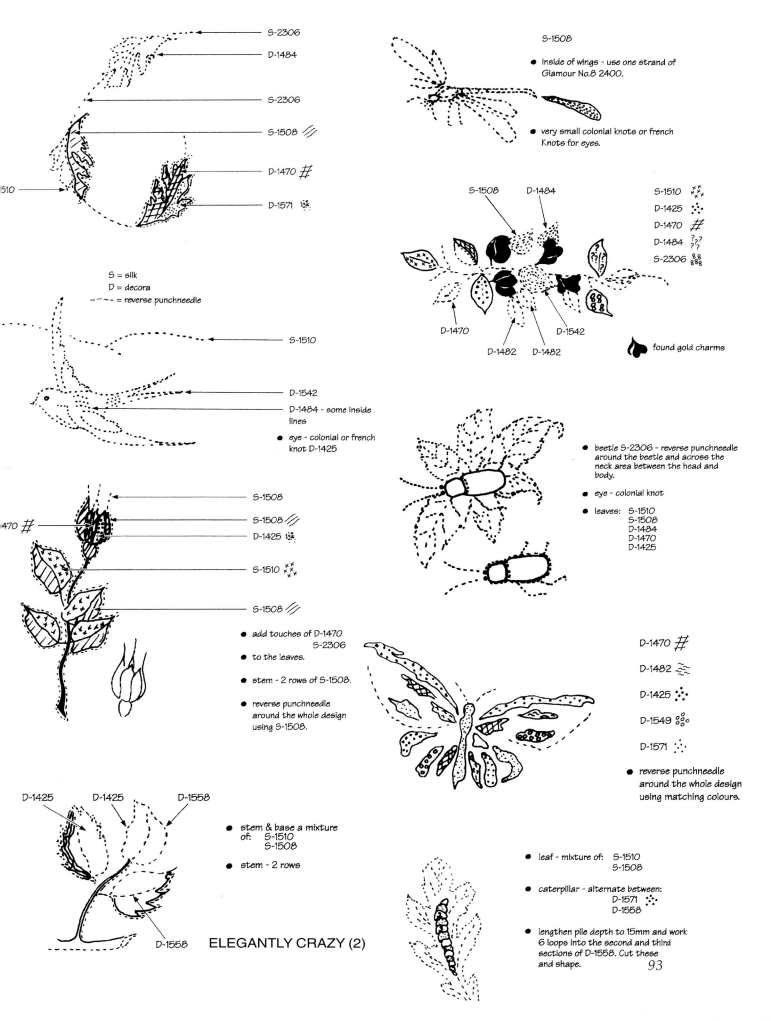

S-2306

D-1484

S-2306

S-1508 ///

D-1470 #

D-1571 ✿

510 →

S = silk
D = decora
- - - = reverse punchneedle

S-1510

D-1542

D-1484 - some inside
lines

● eye - colonial or french
knot D-1425

S-1508

S-1508 ///
D-1425 ✿
S-1510 ✗✗

S-1508 ///

470 #

● add touches of D-1470
         S-2306
● to the leaves.
● stem - 2 rows of S-1508.
● reverse punchneedle
around the whole design
using S-1508.

D-1425   D-1425   D-1558

● stem & base a mixture
of: S-1510
      S-1508
● stem - 2 rows

D-1558

ELEGANTLY CRAZY (2)

S-1508

● inside of wings - use one strand of
Glamour No.8 2400.

● very small colonial knots or french
Knots for eyes.

S-1508   D-1484

S-1510 ✗✗
D-1425 ⋰
D-1470 #
D-1484 ???
S-2306 ⣿

D-1470

D-1482   D-1482

D-1542

found gold charms

● beetle S-2306 - reverse punchneedle
around the beetle and across the
neck area between the head and
body.

● eye - colonial knot

● leaves: S-1510
          S-1508
          D-1484
          D-1470
          D-1425

D-1470 #

D-1482 ≋

D-1425 ⋰

D-1549 ⣿

D-1571 ⋰

● reverse punchneedle
around the whole design
using matching colours.

● leaf - mixture of: S-1510
                     S-1508

● caterpillar - alternate between:
          D-1571 ⋰
          D-1558

● lengthen pile depth to 15mm and work
6 loops into the second and third
sections of D-1558. Cut these
and shape.

93

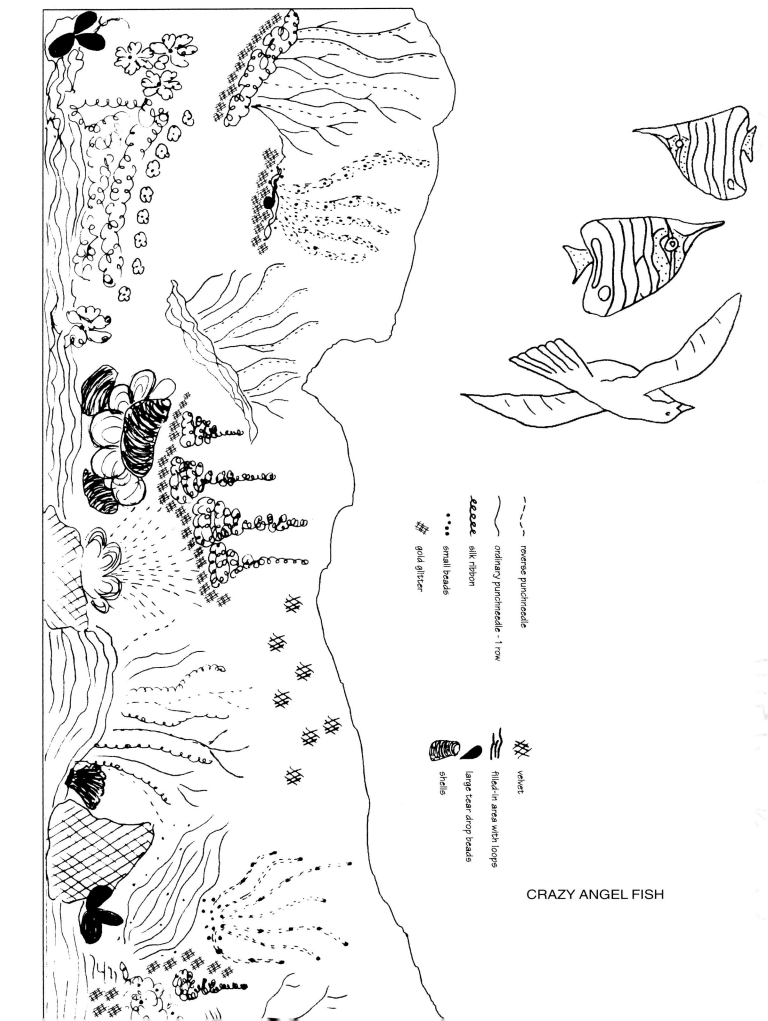

reverse punchneedle

ordinary punchneedle - 1 row

silk ribbon

small beads

gold glitter

velvet

filled-in area with loops

large tear drop beads

shells

CRAZY ANGEL FISH

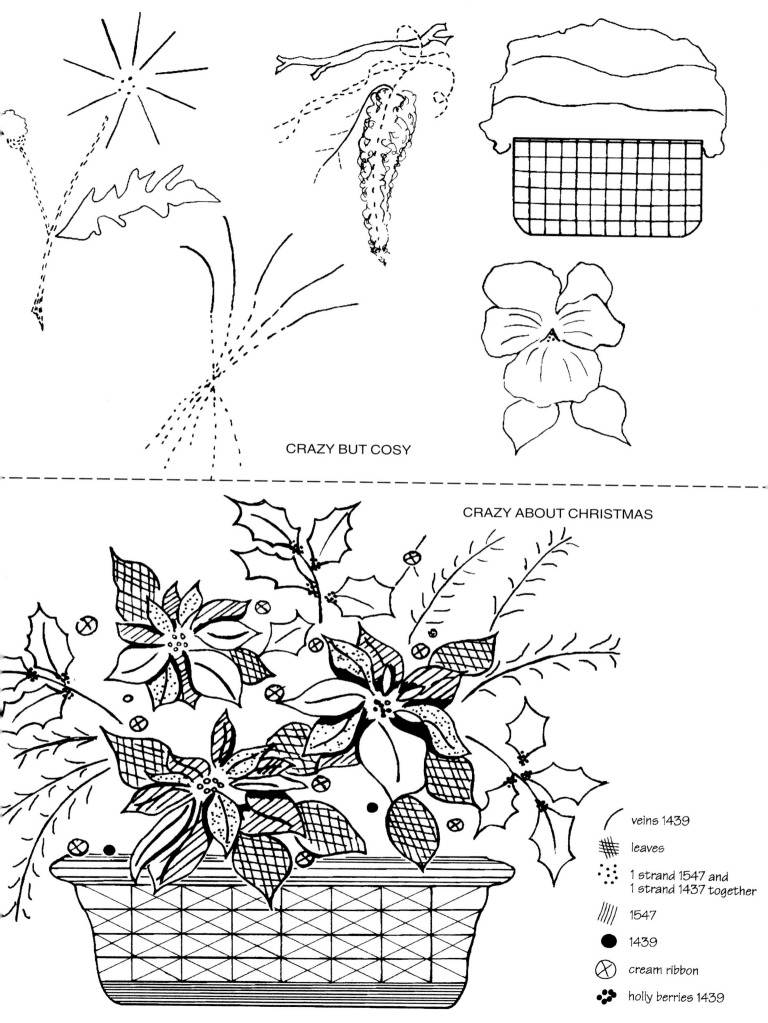

CRAZY BUT COSY

CRAZY ABOUT CHRISTMAS

veins 1439

leaves

1 strand 1547 and
1 strand 1437 together

1547

1439

cream ribbon

holly berries 1439

AUSSIE PUBLISHERS

DISTRIBUTORS

Madeira Australia
25 Izett Street
Prahran Vic 3181 Australia
Tel: +61-3-9529 4400
Fax: +61-3-9525 1172
Email: info@penguin-threads.com.au

Madeira Threads (UK) Limited
York Road, Thirsk
North Yorkshire Y07 3BX UK
Tel: +44-1845-524880
Fax: +44-1845-525046

Margaret Barrett Distributors Ltd
19 Beasley Ave
PO Box 12-034 Penrose
Auckland New Zealand
Tel: +64-9-525 6142
Fax: +64 9-525 6382

Australian Publications
3010 W. Anderson Lane, Suite G
Austin Texas 78757 USA
Tel: +1- 888-788 6572
Fax: +1-512-452 3196
Email: sewmor@aol.com

Quilter's Resource Inc.
2211 North Elston Avenue
Chicago Illinois 60614 USA
Tel: +1-773-278 5695
Fax: +1-773-278 1348

VIDEOS

Jenny Haskins
A Touch of Class — Sewing with Metallic Threads
Over the Top — Decorative Overlocking/Serging

Leisa Pownall
The A to Z of Hand Embroidery
More Embroidery Stitches and Shadow Embroidery
Animals and Flowers in Bullion Stitch
The Wonderful World of Smocking

Eileen Campbell
Machine Appliqué
Basic Free Machine Embroidery
An Introduction to Machine Quilting

Nola Fossey
Creating Wearable Art

Gabriella Verstraeten
Having Fun with Machine Embroidery
Appliqué with a Difference

For more information about punchneedle embroidery, visit Pamela Gurney's website at
www.eisa.net.au/~dndesign

For further details about the equipment used in this book, contact:

Pamela Gurney
Tel: (03) 97120 408
International: +61-3-97120 408
E-mail: *dndesign@eisa.net.au*